To Kate and Tommy

*Things that go bump in the night,
that make the child cry out in fright,
another battle, another fight.
Things that go bump in the night.*

Mary Margaret Doherty

Contents

Chapter 1 Weetabix And The Wobs	3
Chapter 2 Moving Times	14
Chapter 3 Breaking Glass	23
Chapter 4 Shirley Temple	30
Chapter 5 Duty Bound	38
Chapter 6 Girlie Nights	46
Chapter 7 Back Against The Wall	55
Chapter 8 Secret Lives	65
Chapter 9 A Wandering Star	76
Photographs	86
Chapter 10 Burning Things	98
Chapter 11 The Guilt Trip	116
Chapter 12 The Boy	123
Chapter 13 Disappearing World	132
Chapter 14 Petty Crime And Punishment	140
Chapter 15 Give Me The Child Until He Is Seven	150
Chapter 16 A Tale Of Two Mothers	164
Chapter 17 A Dopey Child	178
Chapter 18 The End	194
Afterword	208
About the Author	215

Chapter 1

Weetabix And The Wobs

'Mary, quick, get up, Son and your Daddy are killing each other outside the brewery, we have to go!' roared Teresa.

A bright light was piercing my eyelids, I was almost blind with the sleep, but I jumped from my bed and ran after Teresa who was already down the stairs and opening the front door. I didn't stop to grab shoes or a coat as I raced after her into the dark night oblivious to the cold, though I was shivering uncontrollably. Teresa was running breathlessly toward the end of the street as quickly as the weight of my 3 year old Brother Tommy who she was carrying in her arms would allow. Tommy was crying loudly, his blonde curls were bobbing in the breeze as his head bounced against her shoulder.

It was 1967 and at 4 years old I didn't

understand why my laughing Daddy and my big Uncle Son would be killing each other or even what killing meant; though I knew it was something really bad and my heart thumped in my chest with terror.

The brewery was close, it's colossal chimneys towered above the nearby rows of cramped terraced houses; malevolently puffing out its beer sullied smoke, corrupting the air with a pungent smell reminiscent of Weetabix. Teresa stopped running and turned to wait for me with one hand outstretched; the other arm still gripping Tommy tightly against her chest. She was my Mammy's youngest Sister and barely 10 years of age, but responsibility came early to Traveller girls.

Shouts, cries and screams could be heard from the large crowd of people who had gathered to watch the killing. Teresa, still holding onto Tommy and me, pushed her way to the front. In the centre of the circle of transfixed spectators stood Daddy, slightly crouched, shoulders hunched, iron fists raised ready to strike his much larger, heavy set opponent, Uncle Son who had his back to us and was dancing from side to side preparing to dodge the anticipated furious blows.

'Come on, come on, you big fat Bastard!' snarled Daddy, his teeth bared looked so white against the dark contrast of his black clothes and there was a look in his eyes that frightened me.

'You'll never beat my Sister again you baldy Bastard, I'll kill you!' warned Son.

Then they ran at each other, punching and jabbing, punching and jabbing whilst still doing that strange, obscenely graceful dance.

'Go on Son give it to him!' yelled one man.

'That's enough now boys, will yee stop in the honour of God?' cried another.

One of Son's blows struck Daddy's nose. Blood sprayed upwards, downwards, sideways in both directions. The crowd hushed. My breath caught in my throat; a scream needed to erupt, but became wedged in there too afraid to come out to play. The crowd roared again, Mammy screamed.

'Son, you Bastard leave him alone!'

The two Men stopped dancing. Daddy wiped the blood from his nose with the back of his hand; the same hand that he then curled into a fist. He stared at Son with pure hatred and lashed out with such force that Son was knocked backwards off his feet and onto the ground.

'Get up, you dirty tick, fat Bastard I'm gonna eat the nose off ya!' demanded Daddy.

Son was back on his feet in seconds. Mammy screamed again, loyalties torn.

'Tommy stop, that's enough, stop please God!'

A brave man ran over, and pushed himself between them.

'That's fuckin enough I tell yee; you've

had a fair go, stop now for Jesus sake!' It was the voice of reason from before.

The two combatants cast him aside for his trouble. He stumbled, fell over onto his bottom, but quickly scrambled to safety. No time to waste, grudges to appease, they carried on crashing blows upon each other. I wanted desperately to look away, but couldn't. I wanted Mammy, but couldn't move either. Suddenly the sound of eardrum piercing bells filled the night.

'The Wobs are coming, for fucks sake, you're gonna be lifted!'

The warring men were as deaf to the warning voice as they were to the approaching sirens. Faces covered in blood, eyes and lips puffed and swollen, fists grazed and bleeding; they heard and saw nothing, transfixed by a mutual all-consuming need to destroy the other.

The bells were upon us. Cars and vans came speeding around the corner and screeched to a halt around the violent scene. Men in black helmets and jackets with brass buttons crashed open their vehicle doors, leaping into action. The crowd quickly dispersed, running away in all directions like lambs fleeing a pack of black wolves. Tommy's wails became louder, freeing me from my paralysis. I looked up at him; tears streamed down his small face, his eyes were red, snot poured from his nose. Teresa was shaking and crying too. I broke free of her hand and ran to Mammy.

Two of the men in helmets were wrestling with my Father, trying to pin his arms behind his back. Mammy was weeping and holding onto Daddy's arm trying vainly to push them off and pleading with them not to take him away; so I pleaded too; wrapping my arms around Daddy's leg whilst he was still kicking out trying to prevent the wobs from locking his arms behind him:

'Please, please don't take my Daddy!' I sobbed.

A third officer dragged me from him and pushed me aside. He then ripped Mammy's fingers from her Husband's arm:

'Fucking calm down will you, he'll be alright, just take your kid home; she's bleedin terrified!'

My Father gave up his struggle and they dragged him over to one of the vans, threw him in the back and slammed the door shut.

'You'd better keep your hands off him when you get him in the cell, I'm warning yee!' yelled Mammy.

Uncle Son, still resisting arrest, was also overcome and thrown in another van, but kicked out at one of the officers as he landed in the back. The man fell backwards into the gutter, his helmet flew from his head and bounced into the road, chinking and clinking as it rolled along. We watched until all of the cars and vans were out of sight. Only Mammy and I, Teresa, Tommy and Aunty Eileen, my Mother's older Sister who everyone called Daughter, remained.

'Come on Kate, let's go back to the house and get a sup of tea' she suggested.

Mammy took the still wailing Tommy from Teresa's arms and began to soothe him with kisses and hushes. I took Teresa's hand again as we walked with leaden steps the short distance to our house on Denmark Road. Once indoors we all immediately felt a chill.

'Will we go into the front room and light a fire before we perish with the cold?' asked Daughter.

My Mother opened the door and switched on the light revealing her pride and joy; the new gold vinyl 3 piece suite resplendent with soft, deep gold and brown cushions. Brown and gold flecked vinyl flooring, a gold rug and a gold and glass display cabinet full of fancy ornaments made the room look like a scene from a film.

Teresa got to work building and lighting a

fire. The rest of us flopped heavily on the settee. Tommy was soon sound asleep.

'Teresa take the child to bed will you, then make a drink of tea', said Daughter.

Teresa did as instructed. As soon as Mammy's arms were free of Tommy I nestled next to her. She placed an arm around my shoulder, squeezed me tightly and kissed my cheek over and over. She began weeping, her shoulders gently rising and falling; worried for her I cried too.

'Mammy please don't cry; the man with the helmet said Daddy will be alright!'

'Ah Kate, stall; you're upsetting the child!'

'But Daughter, what if the Wobs corb them in the cells?'

'They won't you mog, forget about it now! What about your man trying to split the two of them up and getting knocked on his arse? A pure gomey!' she added as she began to laugh.

'Then when Son kicked the wob and he

went down on his arse too and his helmet went flying up the road; I taught, ah Mamma, he's done, they'll corb him! But then the policeman got up off his feet, rubbed his arse and carried on about his business!'

Well that was it; the two of them started laughing so hard and couldn't stop. Their faces turned red, they doubled over, groaning and gasping for elusive breath. Teresa walked in, saw the state of them, then looked at me, their laughter was too infectious to resist; we both burst out laughing too.

My Father came home early the next morning and told my Mother the wobs had released him once he'd sobered up, and that he would shake hands with Son the next time he saw him. Then he leaned forward and kissed her on the cheek, she pushed him away playfully and called him a mog. He grabbed her around her waist and waltzed her around the kitchen singing I'll take you home again Kathleen and they both laughed out loud. There was always a lot of laughter in our home; and it was badly needed to soften the many blows.

Chapter 2

Moving Times

I'm a summer person and always have been. The signs of approaching spring, lighter evenings, new buds on trees and early blossoms raise my spirits with their promise of new adventures, challenges and long hot summers ahead. I know I'm not unique in my naive optimism, many others share it too; but it has only recently dawned on me why I'm so season sensitive. Many of my truly happy childhood memories are always bathed in sunshine and linger in my mind long after the actual events occurred; their far reaching rays providing protective warmth against memories of colder, darker times.

Not long after the fight, winter turned the corner into spring and Daddy bounced into the house one day, lifted Tommy and I into his arms, swung us around and announced that he had a great surprise for us. Mammy was all smiles and clearly in the know. We wriggled out of his arms and looked at them both with joyous expectation; maybe it was a load of sweets or new toys, or both? Then he explained that we had to go searching for the surprise and took us from the house and off up the road.

I'm sure Tommy didn't really understand what was going on, but infected by my excitement he held my hand whilst we skipped along with our parents either side of us holding our hands. I felt sure they must have wanted to skip too, but managed to contain themselves. We walked along Princess Road passing through the omnipresent shadow of the brewery into the sunny warmth of 1960s Moss Side. Past the cinema and half way down the endless row of shops we crossed the road and headed towards a huge estate of bay fronted terraced houses. We stopped a few streets in at a junction when my parents were hailed by a man they knew.

'Well hello Kate and Tommy, where are yee two off to?'

Ignoring the man I noticed there were two corner grocer shops facing each other with kids playing noisily outside and bells ringing as people went in and out of the shop doors. A group of small girls were playing hopscotch on the pavement; one of them looked up and smiled at me with sparkling white teeth and huge dark eyes. I grabbed Mammy's hand tighter, I didn't smile back. She looked different, her hair was so long, straight and black and her skin was brown, she made me feel nervous somehow. I was compelled to drag my eyes from her strange face when my parents stopped talking to the man and continued walking.

We began to move down a long street of terraced houses filled with people talking to each other at their doorsteps or sitting on the curb watching children playing on the roads and pavements. There were many faces similar to ours; but many of different colours and shades with weird sounding voices to match. I felt scared and overwhelmed, though I began to relax a little when I saw Mammy and Daddy smiling and nodding at the people, even calling out hellos to a few of them.

Then we stopped in front of a house with a bright red door and Daddy produced a key, with a dazzling white smile he revealed that this was our surprise, a lovely new home. I was gutted, this was the surprise! How in the name of God could a new house compare to sweets and toys or even a trip to Belle Vue (which I had been secretly hoping for). Then he opened the door, ushered us all in, put his arm around Mammy and kissed her cheek. I didn't realize it at the time; but he saw the house as a great move upwards, a huge achievement. However, I did observe that he and Mammy looked very happy, so I began to feel happy too. He took us on a tour of the property and we saw that it had a proper bathroom (which was soon knocked out to make way for an additional bedroom), and even had an air raid shelter in the backyard for future adventures, so it did turn out to be a terrific surprise after all.

The move wasn't taking place until the following week so we returned to the house on Denmark Road. In the interim, my Mother busied herself with packing ready for the move, and dragging her children to shops all over Manchester buying new towels, bedding and black curtains with dramatic red and white rose prints for the window of the posh front room in the new house.

I've often wondered if my Father noted the initial look of disappointment in my eyes that day we first saw Criccieth Street and wanted to compensate for it; as a few days later he woke us by calling up the stairs;

'Mary, Tommy come down the stairs, I've got a surprise for yee!'

I grabbed sleepyhead Tommy by the hand and hurried downstairs. Daddy was standing in the kitchen laughing, whilst holding a white enamel bucket. Mammy was standing with her back leaning against the sink and shaking her head disapprovingly.

'Come here yee two, look what I got yee!' he said as he crouched down and gently placed the bucket on the floor.

Still holding Tommy's hand, we approached the surprise tentatively and peered in.

'They're two little baby chicks; the brown one is for you Tommy and the yellow one is for you Mary. I got them off a farmer in the country, do yee like them?' he asked with his eyes twinkling.

Mammy's emerald eyes were smiling too.

'Oh God Daddy they're beautiful, can we

hold them?' I replied.

He carefully picked them up and placed our chicks on our outstretched cupped hands. Tommy, scared by the sudden movement of his little creature dropped it in his fright and started wailing loudly. But I held on firmly, though gently to my tiny yellow bundle of fluff. I stared into its minute glassy black eyes and stroked its soft downy fur with an index finger. It was gorgeous, I felt so overwhelmed with the need to watch over it, and protect it forever.

Tommy was wary of his and decided he didn't want anything more to do with it. Rejected, his brown chick was placed back in the bucket. I placed mine in there too so it wouldn't be lonely; then spent the whole day cooing and fussing over them. I took great joy in watching them take small hesitant steps on their little spindly legs in the back yard. I made them take plenty of bucket rests just so I had an excuse to cover them with tissue blankets which they tore to shreds with their inquisitive baby beaks. I couldn't get to sleep for ages that night for I was too hyped up with excitement.

Very early the next morning I shrugged off the scant sleep I'd had and skipped downstairs to my vulnerable dependents. I could see my Mother through the kitchen window hanging clothes on the washing line in the back yard. Tommy was dozing on the couch in the living room.

I sat on the floor nearby, reached out for the bucket and pulled it toward me; full of eager anticipation for the joys ahead; but something was wrong, terribly wrong! The small baby chicks were lying unnaturally still at the bottom, no chirps, no twitches, nothing! I reached in and prodded each chick softly with my finger, still nothing! Then Mammy walked in, and as I looked up at her beseechingly, she knew immediately that something was wrong; she crouched down beside me, looked at the still chicks then gently put an arm around my shoulders.

'Ah baby, they're dead, the poor little craters, what happened?'

We both looked up at the sound of Tommy's cries. He slipped off the couch and climbed onto Mammy's lap whilst she was still crouched beside me, hovering over my poor dead chicks.

'I diden mean it Mammy, dey twied to ged away!' he sobbed.

Evidently Tommy's fear of the unknown had been replaced by a rough curiosity. I knew he hadn't killed the chicks deliberately; but in the short time they had been in my life they had quickly instilled in me a new found need to nurture and I was heartbroken and inconsolable in my loss for many a day after.

Chapter 3
Breaking Glass

Back in the 1960s local pubs were often the hub of community life; and it was not uncommon for working class people to meet up in their favourite haunts most nights. My parents were no exception to this; like many Irish Travellers they liked a drink. Teresa babysat Tommy and me every night; and like the dutiful sister she purported to be; would have us settled in bed at a respectable hour. What my Mother and Father didn't know was that as soon as they were out of the way she would drag me from my slumbers as a witness or accomplice to her shenanigans.

Teresa was a bit of a rebel, a defiant minx who didn't care what people thought of her. Her idea of the height of entertainment was to wind people up with her cheek or elaborate practical jokes. Her favourite one was the old milk bottle trick.

By this time we'd been in the new house about a year. The front parlour window had a deep sturdy ledge on the outside with a lamppost located an ideal four feet away directly opposite. She would wait until dark then get an empty milk bottle to which she would tie a long length of black thread around the neck; and I would be made to hold it whilst she tied the other end of the thread around the lamppost. The bottle would then be placed on the window ledge. Laughing guiltily (I at least had the grace to feel guilt!); we would go back indoors, upstairs to the front bedroom and look out the window (peering craftily through the side of the net curtains) waiting in the dark for the first victim to pass. We never had to wait long for some unsuspecting man or woman to walk by, whereupon, the bottle would fall, smash on the pavement and give them an awful fright with the loud crash in the still of the quiet street.

She would sometimes perform this trick as many as four to five times per night. With each victory she'd throw herself on the bed in convulsive fits of laughter; but if some poor soul screamed with shock Teresa would be beside herself with wicked glee and barely able to breathe for laughing so hard. Frequently an irate victim would hammer at the front door knowing the culprit was behind it. Teresa ignored them more often than not; occasionally she would open it, look innocently at them whilst rubbing pretend sleep from her eyes and declare that she'd been sleeping and it must've been the wild boys who lived up the street whose house number she couldn't quite remember.

At the end of many such nights I'd be drifting off to sleep when I'd hear my parents coming home from the pub, sometimes they'd go quietly to bed, more often they didn't and the arguments would start. Teresa and I would crouch at the top of the stairs in the dark ready to leap to Mammy's defence if necessary, and we frequently had to as Daddy was always so full of anger in drink. One incident I recall vividly commenced with him yelling at my Mother:

'Who was that bastard you were talking to at the bar tonight? You fucking whore!'

This onslaught of verbal abuse was quickly followed by the sound of him grinding his teeth, always a very bad sign. Mammy shouted at him to leave her alone; insisting that she'd talked to nobody, that he was a jealous fool and should cop himself on. Then my Father started throwing things at walls, ornaments, cups, glasses were smashed to smithereens. Teresa and I ran downstairs and begged him to stop, but he just roared at us.

'Get up those fucking stairs right now!'

We did, but not before we'd seen Mammy slumped in the chair, even heavily pregnant she was beautiful with her long black hair, green eyes and full lips. Everybody said she was the same as the film star Elizabeth Taylor; but I bet Elizabeth in her whole lifetime never looked as defeated and thoroughly miserable as my Mother did during her many battles with her violent Husband. Back upstairs we heard her scream at him to get off her, and though her screams resonated up and down the quiet street, nobody knocked on the door to make him stop. Teresa and I ran down again and saw him with his fist wrapped around her hair, dragging her about the living room floor whilst she grabbed vainly at his hand to try to free her hair of his vice like grip.

We screamed then too, and this made him stop on that occasion, he stormed from the room and went thundering up the stairs to bed. Leaving us to help Mammy up off the floor, and bathe her puffed, bleeding face whilst sobs wracked her poor battered body.

Other times he would only stop long enough to grab us by the arms, push us through the door, and then place something against it to prevent us going to her rescue again. Tommy never came down the stairs; he always waited at the top whimpering forlornly and crying,

'Mammy, Mammy, Mammy!' over and over again.

Eventually it would end; we'd all go to bed and fall into an exhausted troubled sleep. In the morning after each violent episode we would help Mammy rearrange the furniture, sweep and mop up the broken glass, hair and blood. She would thank us for our help, give us all a kiss and make breakfast. Whenever Daddy came down the stairs and saw the state of her face he would always cry out:

'Oh God Kate no! Oh God I'm so, so sorry, please forgive me darling I promise I'll never, never do it again!'

We all knew he was genuinely deeply

remorseful for what he'd done; but being sorry didn't make it alright; especially as she always forgave him and he did do it again, many, many times over many, many years

Chapter 4

Shirley Temple

The swinging 60s weren't called that for nothing. Even as a very young child I noticed people seemed happier, they smiled a lot, looked out for each other (though they never interfered in family business!), appeared to have a zest for life and were so friendly. They didn't seem to mind (outwardly at least) if others were doing well for themselves and had more than them. Everyone wore their best clothes on Sundays and didn't look too bad the rest of the week either.

Criccieth Street was a truly multi-cultural community. There were Africans, Jamaicans, Scotch, Irish (travellers and non-travellers), Asians, English and Polish people all living side by side, some very poor, some more affluent; all so different in terms of our belief systems, experiences and outlooks. Yet our differences connected us, made us feel the same, it just worked somehow; and so naturally that I didn't even know I was different. I'd soon got over my fear of the dark skinned children; and they became my friends in the street where I would play with them for hours upon hours. I would often go into their houses to eat strange, but delicious foods with unfamiliar and exotic names such as yam, sweet potatoes and curry; or they would come into our home for homemade soda bread, bacon, cabbage and spuds.

Dad was a grafter; he would have died rather than claim benefits or public assistance as it was called then; and the fruits of his labours showed. We had a lorry and a car. A beautiful front parlour decorated with floral wallpaper and furnished with a deep pile carpet, the gold vinyl 3 piece suite (shortly to be replaced by an enormous black leather suite with gold velour cushions), a drinks bar (from which I once sneaked a drink of what I thought was Champagne, only to be violently sick when it turned out to be filled with carpet shampoo!) and the obligatory display cabinet filled with sparkling glasses, china and expensive ornaments. Mammy always dressed fashionably, she had great taste and never wore an outfit that didn't have perfectly matching, colour co-ordinated accessories. We were not spoilt; but my parents ensured that we dressed nicely too, had regular treats, and were bought gifts for Christmas and Birthdays; we wanted for nothing except emotional stability.

The black and white television was the whole family's prized possession and it dominated the living room. Back then broadcasting was limited to just a few channels presenting programmes and movies during evenings and weekend afternoons were spent watching films (or filims as we called them).

Tommy and I adored the old Shirley Temple movies and were thrilled by the escapades Hollywood dreamed up for her.

In the early hours of May 20th 1968 Dad roused Teresa, Tommy and I from our sleep to tell us that Mammy needed to go to hospital to have her new baby and that we would have to go to stay with various members of the family. We were all bundled into the back of his black car, Mammy, very laboriously (her pregnancies were huge) squeezed herself onto the front seat. As the car moved off she turned to us and gave Teresa a crown (5 shillings) me a half crown (2 shillings and sixpence) and Tommy a bob (1 shilling) and told us to be good. We could do a lot of damage to a sweet shop with such riches in those days, so we were all delighted.

Teresa was the first to be dropped off at Mammy's Aunty Katie's house to spend the night with the girls (Katie's young Daughters). Tommy and I were then taken to a three storey house nearby. My Mother stayed in the car whilst Daddy took us through the open front door and rang a bell to the side. We waited in a black and white floor tiled hall, within seconds Uncle Arthur, Mammy's younger Brother and his wife Winnie appeared at the top of a long flight of stairs. Dad took us up to them, explained what was happening then ran down the stairs back out the door to Mammy.

Uncle Arthur and Auntie Winnie took us into their bed with them. Tommy went to sleep almost immediately; but I couldn't settle, I was afraid, worried for my Mother. Why had she given us that money and told us to be good? Was there a chance she wouldn't be coming back? I started to cry and pleaded with Uncle Arthur to take me to Teresa at his Mother's house. He must have felt sorry for me because he did; it wasn't far and I was soon snuggled up between Teresa, Roseleen and Katie's other girls, all in one bed. They were only kids themselves;

but they made me feel secure as they explained that Mammy would be OK; she was just having a baby and would be back home with a new little brother or Sister in a couple of days. I slept like a new born baby myself following their reassurances.

Sure enough, a few days later we were picked up by Daddy, and dropped off back at the house to wait whilst he went to collect Mammy and our new baby Sister from the hospital, we didn't have to wait long as St Mary's wasn't far. We'd been instructed to wait in the front parlour, a room usually out of bounds to us; but one that now befitted the grand occasion of the arrival of a new member of the family. We heard the car pull up outside, then the front door opening; and in walked Mammy, all smiles and looking lovely. We ran to her and she threw her arms around us; smothering our faces with kisses whilst telling us how much she'd missed us.

Daddy was holding a carrycot which he reverently placed on the settee. Mammy gently pushed us forward and told us to have a look at our new Sister, she was gorgeous. Indeed she was, with a tiny porcelain doll like face framed with a mass of perfectly straight, short black hair, I loved her instantly. Mammy asked us what we should call her, without a moment's hesitation I replied,

'Let's call her Shirley'.

Tommy started jumping up and down with excitement.

'Yeah, yeah, let's call her Shirwey Tempil!' he yelled.

Anyone would be forgiven for thinking that the real one had arrived in Moss Side with the level of joy in evidence in our parlour in our home on that day. However, Tommy and I soon became excited about something else; we'd eyed the box of Cadbury's chocolate roses nestled at the bottom of the baby's carrycot and she paled into insignificance by comparison to them. Mammy laughed and passed them to us. I opened the lid, peered into the treasure trove of sparkly, individually wrapped, chocolate sensations and was lost.

Shirley, from that day until the present, has continued to fill the lives of our family (what's left of us) with joy, but also with heartache in equal measures during her eventful life.

Chapter 5

Duty Bound

Shirley was only a few months old when my parents asked the girl next door but one, Christine, to babysit one night. Teresa wasn't around, she must have been very ill indeed to have been spared her nightly duty. Christine was a lovely girl, Tommy and I really warmed to her; though she was only a young teenager and I don't think she'd had much experience of babysitting. We hadn't been in bed long and there wasn't much chance of going to sleep as we could hear Shirley's crying going on and on downstairs. Christine was desperately trying to comfort her, but she was having none of it (even then she was stubborn!). Taking pity on Christine Tommy and I went to her rescue. I was five, Tommy was four, we padded downstairs on our bare feet, walked into the living room and saw Christine close to tears. I lifted Shirley out of her carrycot, placed her against my shoulder and began to rock and soothe her. She stopped crying right away to the immense relief and delight of the harassed babysitter; who showed her appreciation by showering Tommy and I with sweets and pop and by allowing us to stay up late playing with the baby on the settee.

When our parents returned from the pub they weren't cross about us still being up for they knew the score. Paying Christine with thanks and a few bob they sent her home and us off to bed. All was quiet and well as I began to drift off into a contented sleep and then I heard a bang followed by a crash and a scream. Shirley began to wail; I quickly jumped from my bed and ran to my parent's room to her cot to soothe her again. Holding her in my arms I sat on my parents bed; Tommy came in crying, sat beside me and rested his small, blonde head on my shoulder. I desperately wanted Tommy and Shirley to stop crying so that I could hear what was going on downstairs, it had suddenly gone very quiet, though that wasn't necessarily a good thing. I calmed and hushed them both as best as I could.

'Whisht now Tommy, wisht it'll be alright'

His cries soon reduced to a whimper, Shirley was already gently snoring. Then Mammy's voice called up to us,

'Mary, Tommy are yee ok, is the baby alright?'

'Yes Mammy, are you alright?' I answered as a sob caught in my throat.

'Yes baby, but let me give you a piece of advice; never marry a baldy man!'

Oh God, how I wish she had never uttered those word for the violence that followed was devastating.

'You bad bitch, you fucking whore, I'll

kill ya!'

My Father roared as glass smashed, furniture crashed to the floor and my Mother screamed in terror. There was no Teresa to help me stop him, but I knew I had to try. Poor Tommy was hysterical again, I told him to stay where he was, put Shirley back in her cot and went downstairs on legs of jelly to another bloodbath.

The living room door was closed; silence lay heavily in the room beyond. I tried to push it open, but something was blocking it. I pushed harder and it gave a little, providing a gap wide enough for me to squeeze through. The first thing I saw was my Father sitting on his armchair with his head in his hands, he was crying. The second thing I saw was my Mother lying on the floor. Her hair in knotted bunches framed her blood smeared face, her eyes were closed, but they weren't meant to be; they'd been forced shut with swelling caused by brutal blows. I ran to her and knelt beside her, my tears dripped onto her face. She couldn't look at me, though through her bruised, swollen mouth she told me she was alright and asked me to help her up. Daddy didn't look up; I helped Mammy to get up and assisted her up the stairs to bed.

The next morning, her lovely face was unrecognisable, distorted by ugly blue and purple bruises and fat with tender swellings. She ignored my Father's pleas for forgiveness this time; calmly packed a suitcase, dressed herself and her children and left the house. Daddy was too ashamed to stop her. Pushing Shirley in her pram with the suitcase balanced on top, she told Tommy and me to hold onto the handle bars as we left Criccieth Street.

I do not remember the journey, but I do recall arriving at a big house where a kindly woman greeted us at the front door; and showed us to a nice room where she told us we would be safe and could stay as long as we needed to.

Mammy lifted Shirley from her pram, left it and the case in the room, had a few words with the kind woman, and then left the house.

She took us on a short train journey to an office with a big, cold waiting room filled with worried looking people, crying children and phones ringing. When it was Mammy's turn to be seen she had to sit on a hard chair with Shirley on her lap and Tommy and I standing either side of her, before a woman sitting behind a large high desk. Mammy told the woman that she had left her Husband because he had beaten her and she needed help from public assistance. I don't know if she received any help from the woman, but I know she felt ashamed asking for it and embarrassed about how she looked; and how everyone in the waiting room was staring at her; and about having to tell this stranger her business. My Mother was always a proud and private person. It didn't help that the woman didn't seem to care.

A couple of days later a Priest came to see us in the safe house. He was a nice Priest and told Mammy in a gentle tone of voice that he could see she'd had a bad beating, a hard time of it and had obviously suffered. However, her Husband Tommy had been to see him to ask for his help in saving his marriage. Tommy was very sorry for what he'd done and had promised the Priest that he would never hit her again. The Priest told Mammy that it was her duty as a good Catholic Wife to forgive her truly contrite Husband and return to him. My Mother told the priest it was not her duty to be her Husband's punch bag and she was never going back to him. The Priest left after further attempts at Catholic guilt tripping her into returning to Daddy were getting him nowhere.

However, one of God's disciples on earth wasn't to be so easily defeated; determined to win on behalf of God, the Pope, his church, and himself he disclosed the safe house location. The very next day, the kind lady didn't look so kind when she knocked on our room door and tight lipped, informed Mammy that her Husband was at the front door; and was refusing to leave until she went down to talk to him.

Mammy had no real choice; she left us in the room and went down to see him. Whatever Daddy said to her was enough to convince her to go back to him. It was the first, but by no means the last time that God, the Pope, his church, the local Priest and my Father would win.

Chapter 6

Girlie nights

Long before Tesco's, Asda, Morrison's et al were even a twinkle in the eye of some greedy entrepreneur; milk was delivered daily, coal weekly; and soft drinks by the Pop man a couple of times per week, but it was the local corner grocer shops that dominated the neighbourhood. We had two on Criccieth Street facing each other on opposite corners, with plenty of business for both. Tick (credit) was readily available for those who needed it. One shop was owned by an Asian family and Teresa gave the Father who ran it the majority of the time, no end of torment. My parents had instilled the importance of politeness and good manners into us; but Teresa wasn't their child and passed no heed to them at all, she just did her own thing.

I witnessed one particular incident of harassment which made me blush to the roots of my hair! We'd entered the shop, setting off the warning tinkle of the doorbell. The shopkeeper looked up with a ready smile on his face to greet his next customer. However, the smile slipped from the poor man's face melodramatically when he saw Teresa entering.

'Hello Sur I've come to buy an orange please' said Teresa, warmly and politely.

Looking worried, perhaps sensing the calm before the storm, he told her to pick any orange she wanted, with what sounded to me like a slight tremor in his voice.

'I don't mean to be cheeky or notten Sur, but I'd be awful glad if you'd pick one for me on account of you knowing your oranges?' she asked sweetly.

The man kindly came around the counter and picked one for her; which wasn't quite right as it wasn't big enough. He had to repeat the process four or five times until he picked the largest orange he could find and she was finally satisfied.

'That's perfect Sur, tanks very much' declared a delighted Teresa as she handed over cash.

I followed her as all smiles she made her way over to the exit. The shopkeeper had visibly relaxed by this point; probably thanking his lucky stars that he'd got off so lightly this time. But as Teresa opened the door setting off the familiar tinkle of the bell, she turned to him:

'It's still not big enough ya bastard!' she yelled as she launched the orange at the beleaguered man's head then legged it.

I stood in shock, rooted to the spot in the doorway. The shopkeeper pushed passed me; almost knocking me over in his haste to catch his eleven year old adversary; but she was already way down the street and rounding a corner, he had no chance! Furious, he faced me:

'Tell that bloody cheeky girl not to come in my bloody barstard shop ever again!' he demanded as he slammed the door in my face.

The opposite corner shop was owned by an elderly couple named Tom and Mary; who knew everyone in the neighbourhood by their first names, and my frequent visits to their establishment holds far more pleasant memories in my mind. On an almost daily basis my Mother would send me there with a list of the groceries she needed. However, as I couldn't read and write Mammy would just tell me what she wanted and I would memorise the items to the complete delight of Tom and Mary who never ceased to be amazed by my powers of recall.

'How can you remember all those things Mary dear when you're only six and can't read?' they would ask every time I went in.

They clearly had a soft spot for me, for when it was my Birthday they presented me with a lovely box of malteser chocolates.

I didn't like being uneducated and was desperate to go to school, but Mammy said I had to wait for Tommy to turn five in September 1969, although I would be almost six and a half, she had reasoned that it was better for us to start together. Over the following summer months my Mother stayed in on Thursday nights; and when Tommy and Shirley were asleep she would come and get me from my bed, take me downstairs, wash my long hair in the kitchen sink, then Platt it whilst we sat on the settee watching This Is Your Life with Eamon Andrews on the black and white television. I loved those girlie nights so much; I had Mammy all to myself for a few hours, nobody knocked on the front door, there were no phones to be ringing; and nobody to cause trouble at least for a few precious hours every Thursday.

She would tell me about her life growing up as a young traveller girl in Ireland with strange customs and a secret language, the cant, developed to prevent the fiercely distrusted country people (non-travellers) from understanding what they were discussing. Having grown up with it, I was of course privy to the secret. If Travellers wanted to do something without alerting others to what they were up to (take something or talk about a non-traveller) they could freely, and often very brazenly, do so in the person's presence thanks to the cant. This language/dialect had been passed down through many generations, and as most Irish Travellers cannot read and write the spellings of the words are of no consequence to them, instead sounds and meanings are everything. For example, soonik the lackeen's reeb it's tome, translates as: look at the girl's hair it's lovely. So, soonik = look, lackeen = girl, reeb = hair, tome = lovely/beautiful. Other examples are: beur = woman, suebler or feen = man, gomey or mog = fool/idiot, galleune =

shock/dismay, stall = stop/wait/hold back, mistle = go/move on, wobs = police, knawk = steal/take, bug = give/pass to/or steal, corb = beat/fight, gammy = bad/no good or loose morals, lurkey = insane, mentally unstable or odd. Though with the exception of the odd word used for descriptive effect, we all spoke the Queen's English amongst ourselves.

On these nights spent with my Mother she told me of the time when she was a teenager when she'd been asked to enter the Rose of Tralee beauty contest by one of the organisers when he'd spotted her at a local market. Her parents would not have allowed this of course, for she would never have been permitted to be paraded in front of country people for fear of them whisking her off to a life of cultural exclusion from her own people. She'd laughed when she'd pointed out that the man wouldn't have been so keen for her to enter the competition anyway if he'd known she was a

Tinker!

Mammy had told me about her family coming to England when she was fifteen so the men could find work in the big cities, and of how they had to live in rooms in boarding houses instead of trailers to be close to the work; and of how alien that had been to her for a long time.

Mammy explained that she knew it was her fault that at age six I would be starting school late; but to make it up to me and to ensure I wasn't at a complete disadvantage from the other children who had a head start on me, she would teach me to write my whole name, and she did; with painstaking patience over the following weeks. She told me over and over that even though we were travellers; and most couldn't read and write, she wanted her children to be able to and to have a chance of a better life.

September finally arrived; Tommy and I were very excited about starting school and thanks to Mammy, I was a little more confident than I would have been if she hadn't taught me to write my name. This achievement was all the more remarkable as my Mother could not read and write herself! She must have asked someone who could to write my name down for her and then memorised it so that she could teach her daughter; it would have made her proud to be able to do that. I could see that pride shinning in her eyes on our first day of school when she looked at Tommy and I, all scrubbed up and wearing matching white pullovers with red piping:

'Yee both look tome' she said with a warm smile as she led us from the house towards a new chapter of our lives.

Chapter 7

Back Against The Wall

As we entered the school playground the first thing that caught my eye were the enormous coloured paintings that covered the back wall depicting children in various poses and engaged in many acts of play. The wall appeared to be fifty feet tall to me, and I would come to know it well. There were hopscotch squares and numbers marked out on one area of the ground and another had a pile of giant hoola hoops waiting forlornly for children to make them feel loved again.

Parents and children crowded near the gates, Mums chatting and gossiping whilst their offspring jumped up and down impatiently beside them or ran ahead to play in the grounds. Holding Tommy and I firmly by our hands, my

Mother ignored them all and made a path through them to the front entrance; we passed through the door into the main hall just as an ear splitting bell rang out making Tommy and me jump in alarm. Mammy walked straight up to a rather stern looking woman, though when she spoke her voice was surprisingly soft and kind.

'Hello Mrs Doherty this must be Mary and Tommy? You can leave them with me, they'll be fine' she said warmly.

My Mother released our hands, bent down to our level and put her arms around us.

'Alright yee two, be good, I'll be back for yee at tree o'clock, OK?'

She had tears in her eyes and I was suddenly desperate for her not to go! I didn't want us to be abandoned in this alien environment, though I said nothing as I didn't want to add to her obvious distress or make Tommy panic. As the woman led Tommy and me away, I turned my head to look over my shoulder at Mammy, and she did the same as she approached the main exit door; I saw a lonesome tear roll down her cheek, she gave me a little wave, and was gone.

My heart sank, but I followed the woman obediently. She took us to the doorway of a large room filled with big windows, desks and chairs and gently pushed Tommy through the opening.

'There you go Tommy, this is your new class now be a good boy'.

Tommy threw a brief frightened glance, accompanied by a wobbly lower lip in my direction before his teacher hustled him quickly to a desk. The woman walked on with me down a long gloomy corridor, and came to a stop outside another classroom:

'And this is your new class Mary; don't look so worried, I'm sure you will fit in just fine'.

The room was full of children my age. The teacher looked at me, I looked back at her, nobody was talking, the eyes of all the children were on me, I could feel their inquisitive rays burning my cheeks, which were hot with embarrassment. This wasn't what I had expected, not at all. In my many daydreams of school life everyone I met would be welcoming and smiley and all would like me instantly. I would have hundreds of new friends and endless sunny days filled with games and exciting adventures! I dragged my eyes away from the still silent teacher to look at my new classmates, and saw a sea of hostile and superior expressions, a few of them giggled. I wanted to run from there, back down the gloomy corridor, out of the door and school gate, catch up with Mammy and tell her that it was OK, I didn't need to go to school after all; I could stay at home with her forever and help her with the house and Shirley! Then the teacher finally broke her silence:

'It's Mary isn't it? Well what are you waiting for dear? Find a seat and settle in'.

I spotted an empty chair, the only one I could see, and wouldn't you know it, right at the back of the room, and next to a mean, brutish looking boy who was literally scowling at me, knowing I would have to sit next him and clearly not happy about it. I made my way towards it on wobbly legs with my eyes cast down to the floor. I sat heavily on the chair behind my little desk. I looked up tentatively and found to my horror that all of the children had turned in their seats to stare at me. My face burned with humiliation, eggs could have been fried to perfection on my flaming cheeks.

'Right, turn around you lot, that's enough gawping, she's just a new girl!' demanded the teacher. She then walked up to me, placed a blue card covered note book, a pencil, a ruler, and a rubber on my desk.

'Please write your name on the front cover Mary, you do know how to write your name don't you?' she asked.

'Yes Mrs, me Mammy learned me how to do it Mrs' I replied nervously, but with a secret sense of pride.

'Mary, you must call me Miss not Mrs, and it's your Mother taught you, not learned you how to write your name' she said.

Well that set the children off giggling and staring all over again. I looked down at my notebook and with a shaky hand, set about the task of writing my name on the front cover. I pressed too hard on the nib of the pencil and it broke off; I was mortified and just stared stupidly at the essential, but now damaged instrument of learning. The boy next to me raised his arm, I turned to stare at him stupidly too:

'Miss, miss, she's broken her pencil already!' he declared gleefully.

'Oh Mary, come up here to the front and I will sharpen it for you, you silly girl!'

Was there to be no end to the torture? I

wondered morosely. I walked to the front of the class and handed her my pencil with a trembling hand, as she returned it to me I said:

'Tanks very much Mrs, I mean Miss' then I ran back to my seat, yet more giggling followed this. The rest of the morning was a blur of letters and numbers pouring from the mouth of the teacher whilst she simultaneously drew the symbols she was talking about with white chalk on a large squeaky blackboard.

When the horrible bell rang again she told us all that it was break time and to go out to play. I followed my classmates into the corridor now filled with all the other little people from other classes and into the playground. I soon spotted Tommy running around playing with a group of boys, it made me smile seeing him so happy, however, the smile quickly slipped from my face when children began bumping into me, I was clearly in the way.

'Move out of the way dopey!' one of them

yelled.

I made my way over to the wall to safety and stood with my back leaning against it. Mostly I looked at the ground, but occasionally I would look up to see all those children, so many of them, laughing, skipping; having great fun, and I longed to be a part of it. However, it was not to be, I stood with my back against the wall during every break time for many weeks to come. At home I never mentioned my suffering to my parents. Every evening I spent ages in the tin bath in the kitchen scrubbing myself extra clean as I was convinced that I must smell bad and that was why none of the children liked me.

Then one ordinary day that started out just like all the others, everything changed. Leaning with my back against the wall, eyes cast downwards as usual; by that stage I no longer felt inclined to look at others enjoying themselves when I was lost in my self-pitying world of forced isolation, I heard a small voice:

'Hiya, what's your name? I'm Margaret; do you want to play with me?'

She was small and thin with a mop of short, straight brown hair, and had a stream of snot running from one nostril to her upper lip which she promptly sniffed up (I would discover later that she constantly had a stream of snot running from one favoured nostril which she was forever sniffing up, but I never minded); and that was it, I had a friend, which meant I wasn't some sort of leper and led to me making another friend, then another until I became part of a large group of friends, and finally accepted after weeks of abject misery. And there started the lesson, not only did I begin to enjoy classes with a new found thirst for knowledge, but more importantly, for me at least, I learned that to belong, to be accepted by your peers is crucial for developing self-esteem. If a person is deemed worthy of being friends with others they must be OK and good to be around. I treasured this hard won knowledge greedily.

So when my cousin Sandra (Auntie Eileen's daughter who was 9 months younger than me) started at my school a few weeks later and I saw her alone at the wall on her first day, I left her there. Though I frequently looked over in her direction guiltily, I was terrified of being excluded again if I talked to a new girl. It was one of my few truly selfish actions in my life, and one I've never forgotten. Though I loved Sandra dearly, I was only six years old and just couldn't bear the thought of being back against the wall.

Chapter 8
Secret Lives

Criccieth Street was a long, broad road filled with people from diverse backgrounds. Most led simple uncomplicated lives; their stories transparent to all who cared enough to see. Others lived closed existences behind shut doors, and permanently drawn curtains. No one would pass comment on the sprinkling of houses where people were rarely seen coming and going and in whose windows lights seldom shone.

At the end of our block of the Street in the corner house, next to what we called the croft (a piece of waste land where three to four houses were believed to have once stood), there lived an African woman and her daughter. The Mother was very dark skinned, voluptuous and always dressed in fabulously colourful traditional African women's costumes with matching flamboyant headdresses wrapped expertly around her glamorous head. Fancy cars would regularly pull up outside her door; each vehicle would have a different African male behind the wheel. The woman would come out to greet them with a smile dazzling enough to match her outfits. Her many suitors would always step out of their cars and hold the door open for her; the engine would sometimes be revved a few times for a little extra aplomb and off they'd go. These exhibitions would often be followed by caustic comments from tight lipped women sweeping their steps or cleaning their windows:

'She likes her fancy men that one!' or:

'Thinks she's a lady, but I bet she's not wearing any knickers under those sheets she calls dresses!'

When she wasn't gadding about with 'one of her fancy men!' the woman would occasionally let her daughter play out on the street with the other children. She was a tall, gangly shy girl who didn't talk much; though as she was cooped up alone in her house a lot of the time she probably didn't have much to say, but how she loved to play. Her huge dark eyes would light up and she would throw her head back and laugh out loud when we played blind man's bluff or tiggy it.

One day we were playing happily together when yet another car pulled up on the Street, and her Mother appeared at the front door holding a suitcase. A man leaped from the car, took the case from her and loaded it in the boot. The woman glared at her daughter:

'Get in de house right away!' she demanded.

My friend with her head lowered followed the order, and as she entered her virtual prison, her Mother pushed her through to the hallway just to speed things up a bit. She then slammed the door shut after her, got in the car with the man and he drove off. I waited until the car disappeared from view then knocked on the door, but there was no answer, so I lifted the letterbox and spoke through the opening:

'It's me, Mary are you alright? Where's your Mammy goin'? When will she be back?' I asked anxiously.

'I am OK, but I cannot open de door. My Mother has gone to Africa for a holiday she be back one month from now. She has done this many times before, I be OK, but please I beg you do not tell anyone!' she replied.

I called every day after that and she did open the door to sneak me in every time. I would share my sweets and pop with her. Her Mother always left her plenty of food when she went on her holidays, but my friend had to do everything for herself, cooking, cleaning, and laundry. She told me that when she was alone, when I wasn't with her she read a lot, about places in the world that she would only visit in her dreams. She was never allowed to go out at all during these periods not even to school. I kept my promise and never told anyone about her secret; though I'm certain now that many adults in the Street must have suspected that a child was home alone, unsupervised for long periods of time, but did nothing about it.

The burden of my secret and my concerns for my friend must have played heavily on my mind for on a few nights during that period I would be woken by the sounds of forlorn wails, what sounded to me to be the cries of a small child and was convinced that one of the Asian families who lived on the Street behind ours had locked their little daughter out in the backyard for some minor misdemeanour. Tormented and exhausted after a few sleepless night, and convinced that all foreign parents treated their offspring abominably I caved in and blurted it out to my Mother, demanding that something be done about the poor child being locked out at night. Mammy chuckled and told me it was just cats making the racket that they sounded like children crying only when they were on the prowl and up to no good at night.

Somebody else prowling for trouble and up to no good day or night was Fred who lived a few doors down from us. He mercilessly beat his poor wife Mary at least twice weekly; her screams could be heard reverberating up and down the back entry. Fred was a big strapping, surly man; Mary was tiny in comparison, and pitied by all on the Street.

'It's a sin what that big Bastard does to that poor crater for notten at all!' I overheard my Mother saying to Auntie Eileen on one occasion.

'I know, Tommy wouldn't lift a hand to you sober, but that animal tortures that poor little woman all the time!' agreed Daughter.

I played with Fred and Mary's children, so I knew the family well, as in our home, what went on behind closed doors stayed there. The subject was never discussed, nobody went to Mary's rescue and over 40 years later the couple remained together until Mary's death a few years ago.

By stark contrast, the neighbours next door to our right seemed normal and happy. There was never a raised voice from either parent and their son Dominic appeared to have it all. They were a lovely family and Tommy and I were always warmly welcomed with an open invitation to play with Dominic and his endless collection of toys and gadgets whenever we wanted to. I don't know if it was because I secretly envied Dominic or if it was due to witnessing the violence in my home or if I just wanted nice things too, but it was around this time that I developed a secret life of my own.

It began the first time my teacher asked me to get her some pencils from the class storeroom. I walked into the store and was greeted by an Aladdin's cave of goodies. There were trays and boxes filled with coloured pens, pencils, crayons, scraps of sparkly material, exercise books, sticky coloured labels and coloured cards. I reached for the pencils for Miss; I picked up a handful then quickly put them back. Lifting my skirt I pulled the top of my woolly tights out, grabbed a handful of the coloured pencils and stuffed them in then added a bunch of bright scraps of fabric and pulled my skirt back down. Returning to the classroom I handed miss her pencils without making eye contact.

For the rest of the day I fidgeted in my seat as I was being prodded by the pencils and the fabric scraps were making my skin itch horribly. I couldn't' wait to get home that day. I raced up to my room and pulled my stolen treasure from my tights and placed it lovingly in a drawer.

After the first time it was easy. As the

children in our class were allowed to go into the storeroom whenever we needed something; and I always needed a lot of somethings!

A few weeks later I had amassed a huge collection of stationary; Daddy asked me one day where I was getting all the pens and pencils from; I told him that the school gave it to all the children so that we could do our homework, he believed me too.

However, one dreadful day put an end to my life of secrets and lies. My teacher suddenly announced one afternoon that a great deal of stock was going missing from the storeroom, and informed us that all the children in our classroom would be searched at the end of the day before going home. At this point I had already been for my daily plunder and my stolen booty felt hot against my skin, as if it would burn a hole right through to my soul for being such a bad, bad girl. My face stung with shame, if the other kids found out just how bad

I really was they would surely march me back against the wall if not out of the school gates forever; then me Mammy and Daddy would kill me!

I asked Miss if I could go to the toilet, nearly fainted whilst I had to wait for what seemed forever for her permission. When I reached the toilet I locked myself in one of the cubicles; then with legs like jelly, and trembling hands I moved aside the lid of the toilet cistern, proceeded to pull all of the evidence out of my tights and stuffed it in there. After replacing the lid I splashed my sizzling face with cold water, and returned to my class.

I had heart palpitations for the rest of the day until the bell rang when I along with the rest of my class were searched. I have never forgotten the profound relief I felt when I took my mother's hand that day and set off for home. I'd had such a lucky escape; I thanked Jesus in my head all the way home and promised him over and over that I would be a good girl for the rest of my life, a promise I couldn't always deliver on!

Chapter 9

A Wandering Star

For Roman Catholics (and all Irish Travellers are Christened in the faith, although many today have found Jesus in other ways by becoming born again Christians, often to keep them off the Demon drink!); the first Holy Communion, especially for girls, is an event of monumental proportions. Back in the 1960s and early 70s children made theirs aged seven. The build up to the special day seemed to go on forever and school life buzzed with an air of excited holiness. Teachers went on incessantly with talk of how blessed we children were with the forthcoming privilege of taking the body of Christ for the first time. The great honour would put us on the righteous road to salvation, of true acceptance by God himself; though the final stamp of approval by the all-powerful one didn't come until we were confirmed, usually around the age of eleven. But all I could think about morning, noon and night was the beautiful white dress with matching white shoes, socks, gloves, veil and a sparkling tiara that I was going to wear on the day.

My Parents took me one Saturday afternoon to choose my Fairy Princess outfit to a shop filled with girlish dreams. The woman who served us treated me like a Princess, as she fussed and oohed and ahed over me. I tried on loads of dresses and loved them all, but it was my Mother who selected the winning one, and it was a stunner. It had a close fitting bodice embroidered with silver threads and a liberal covering of diamante stones. The skirt was full and floor length with layers of satin and taffeta, finished off with a huge white satin sash around the waist. I couldn't stop smiling as we went on to pick my accessories to match my perfect dress and Daddy paid the woman a small fortune for it all. As we left the shop I don't think my feet touched the ground once on the journey home.

However, it was not all good news, before the big day arrived there was a grizzly task that had to be completed, the first confession! In preparation for the taking the body of Christ in the form of a small wafer of bread like substance placed on your tongue to melt (never chewed as befits the Heavenly morsel!). Catholics had to go to confession to admit to all their sins.

The way it works is you go to Church before mass, usually on a Saturday afternoon where imposing confessional boxes stand ominously waiting with two closed doors. The Priest waits behind one of them and the sinner enters to sit upon a stool and face a partition with a small window covered in mesh to disguise you from the priest. He's not supposed to look at you, for the whole ceremony is shrouded in anonymity; so he will sit sideways, and wait for the sinner to say:

'Bless me Father for I have sinned; and it's been 2 years or 6 months etc. since my last confession'

Then the good gentleman replies with words to the effect of:

'Go on my child confess your sins'.

The thing is, you could quite clearly see each other if you dared to look, and everyone knew the parish priests by their voices anyway; and you just knew they recognised your voice too! But it was a charade always worth playing because no matter what you confessed to, as long as you were truly contrite, you were absolved of your sins, big or small. You were given a penance of saying a few prayers (or the whole Rosary if you were really bad!), and that was it, the slate was wiped clean and you could start afresh in the eyes of the Lord!

Well, all of this wasn't fully explained to me, or if it was I didn't listen properly, and my nerves were so bad at the prospect of having to confess to stealing at school and my duplicity in the milk bottle tricks. I heard nothing, but my own guilty thoughts telling me that my black soul was going straight to the bottomless pit when I died; and there was no way the priest was going to let me wear my lovely dress and take the body of Christ into my sinful mouth on the Holy Communion day.

So when Mammy led me to the confessional box, opened the door and gently pushed me forward, my legs were shaking so badly I stumbled, and fell off the stool onto my guilty arse! I picked myself up, sat on the stool and stared at the mesh window with eyes as big as golf balls.

'Do you have anything to confess to my child?' asked the Priest in a voice warped with many years of overindulging in cigarettes and whiskey. But how did he know I was a child, he wasn't looking at me? Oh sweet Jesus, did he know who I was? Would he tell Mammy and Daddy what I'd done if I confessed? But I was trapped and there was nothing I could do except fess up:

'Bless, bless me Father for I have sinned loads and honest to God, on me Mammy's life I'm awful sorry, and I won't ever do it again!'

I was sure the Priest laughed, though as he quickly cleared his throat I thought I must have been mistaken.

'Tell me what you've done child?'

His voice was so kind and gentle, it was my downfall. I started babbling, telling him about stuffing my tights with ill-gotten gains, how I'd nearly got caught, which had stopped me in my tracks; and about the milk bottle tricks, although I conceded that my Auntie is older and should have known better; but if I'd been a good girl I should have tried to stop her. I finished with a sob that stuck in my throat and was sure it would choke me, and would, I was certain, have been a fitting penance for my wickedness.

'You've been a very bad girl indeed, but if you're truly sorry God will forgive you. Are you sorry for the terrible things you've done?' asked the Priest.

'Oh yes sir Father I'm almighty sorry, may God strike me down if I'm lying!' I declared.

'Then say five our Fathers and five Hail Mary's, off you go now and try to be a good girl, God will be watching!' he cautioned.

And that was that, I was forgiven. I walked out of the box feeling pure and clean and promised myself that I'd double up on the prayers the good Father had given me to recite as penance, just to be on the safe side.

The big day finally arrived and as I walked with my family to the church we were bathed in sunshine, my dress and tiara bedazzled passers-by who all smiled and waved at me. One jolly looking man stopped us to give me half a crown, I thanked him and popped it in my little white satin bag; it clinked as it hit the full crown my Mammy and Daddy had already given me. I couldn't believe my luck, not only did I get to be a Princess for the whole day, but family and perfect strangers would give me money too!

At the church all the Holy Communion kids were given a mini bible and a set of white Rosary beads by the Nuns; and when we reached the alter, one by one we were blessed by the Priest as he placed the wafer on our tongues. I remembered not to chew, allowing it to melt in its own good time made it even more special, brought me closer to God.

After the ceremony we were taken to the church hall for a celebratory party where I obtained a belly full of goodies and a bag stuffed with money, it was marvellous. When we arrived home it was still early so Tommy and I and a few of our friends wandered the Streets for a few hours; and as more children joined us wanting to bask in my glory I was like the Pied Piper of Moss Side, minus the pipe.

Our first stop was at the Jamaican shop on the next Street up from ours. On summer days like those they would have huge slabs of ice on a long trestle table outside the shop; and for a few pennies the Jamaican men would shave the ice into a paper cup and fill it with raspberry or cherry juice, they were delicious. With my takings from the day I treated us all to a few of each flavour; one of mine went all over the front of my dress, but I didn't fret for I knew Mammy would scrub it clean and white again.

Walking in the sunshine drinking our slushes on our way to the adventure playground we heard a voice singing loud, the voice was deep and gravelly:

'I was born under a wandering star; I was born under a wandering star, a wanderin', wanderin' star....'

The man didn't stop walking as he sung, I stared after him as he staggered up the road, hypnotised by him. When I told my Mother about him later she told me that the song he was singing was from the movie Paint your wagon, and the man was the double of the movie's star, Lee Marvin. She also told me that the man was an alcoholic, which meant that the poor crater was ruined with the drink. But then with a twinkle in her eye she cupped my face in her hands and told me that on my very special day me and old Lee were both wandering stars. Mammy always had a way with words, and I went to bed that evening feeling like a star.

My parents with me, Birmingham 1963

Mary Margaret Doherty

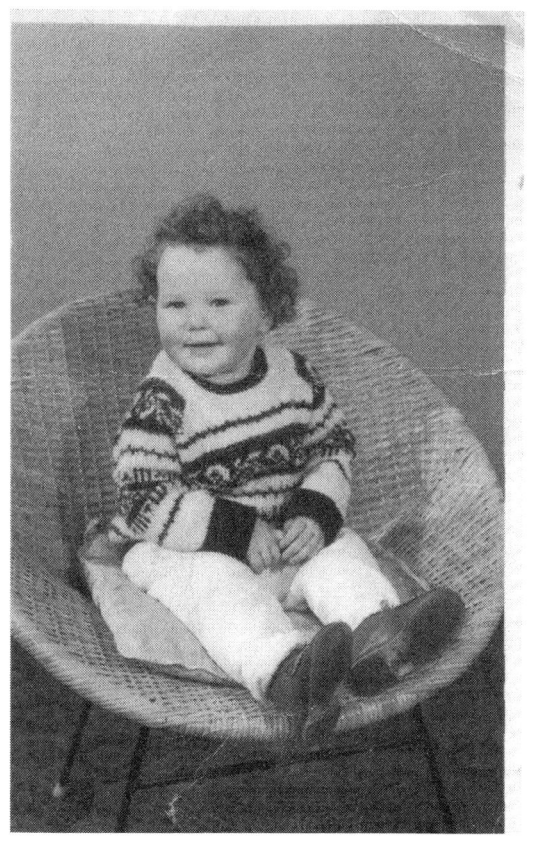

Me aged 14 months, Moss Side 1964

Gyppo

Me aged 3 with my Father, Moss Side 1966

My Father, Tommy, me and Teresa (back of photo) Denmark Road, Moss Side 1966

Daddy with Tommy and Shirley, Criccieth Street 1968

Daddy with Shirley

Mammy with Shirley

My parents with Shirley

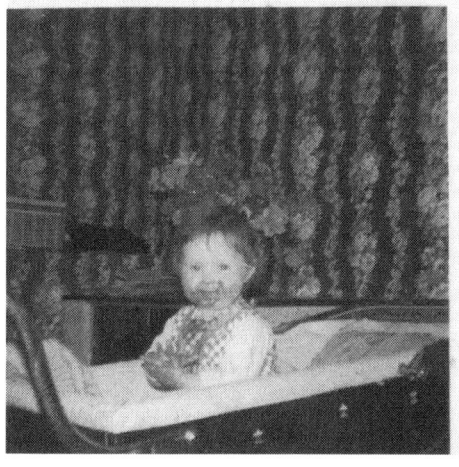

Shirley aged 1

Tommy aged 5

Shirley 1969

Me with Caren, Criccieth Street, summer 1970.

Daddy, Tommy and Shirley Christmas 1970

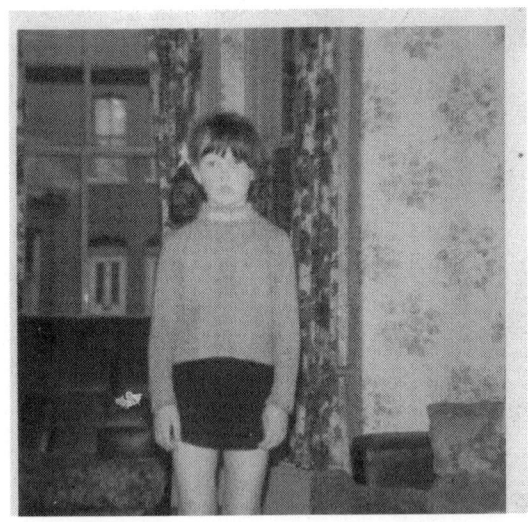

Me 1970 Criccieth Street

**Tommy, Sandra, me, Caren and Shirley
Criccieth Street, summer 1971**

Mago shortly before her death

Grandad Arthur, Nanna Ellie with Sandra and Caren outside the Prince of Wales Pub, Moss Side, 1972

Me, Mammy, Shirley, Teresa, and Tommy Nantwich Road 1973

Daddy, Shirley, Mammy, Nantwich Road 1973

Chapter 10

Burning things

Manchester winters were freezing; the cold would literally chill your bones. The old terrace houses had no central heating, so the only way to get warm was to make fires which took an age to build and set alight. The flames, weak at first, would tentatively flick their tongues into the almost glacial air creating plumes of dense smoke which bumped chaotically into the clouds of hot breath coming from our mouths. It was mesmerising to watch the fires rise in confidence, their warmth caressing our faces making them feel all hot and tingly. Most of the rooms had fireplaces and my parents always tried to ensure that we had plenty of stocks of chopped up bundles of wood and coal in; though in really harsh winters there were many nights when we ran out of supplies.

Tommy had his own room, baby Shirley was in my parent's room, and I shared with Teresa. We would layer the bed with sheets, blankets and coats, anything to generate some heat. We were allowed to build fires in our own room, though as we only had a limited supply of wood and coal we would have to throw old shoes and boots on the fire to keep it alight, they were great, they'd burn hot and bright for ages. Sometimes we'd get sleepy Tommy from his bed to let him snuggle up. Poor Tommy would pay a high price for his comfort when Teresa would tell us grisly ghost stories, making him more chilled than ever. I recall one story that caused shivery fingers of fear to creep up my spine and tousle my hair malevolently:

Toward the end of the nineteenth century a travelling circus was passing through a small village in Ireland when one of the horses stumbled whilst pulling a tent wagon and hurt his leg; but as luck would have it a farmer was going by on his cart with the local vet who promptly tended to the beast's injury, which wasn't as severe as expected, though the vet gave instructions that the horse needed to rest up for a few days. The circus owner was so grateful he decided to set up camp in the nearby field and offered a free show for all the villagers.

The next day the village buzzed with excitement as news spread, for nothing much happened in their sleepy little Hamlet. As the frosty evening grew dark, the locals wrapped up in their warmest coats and headed out to the field of bright lights and rousing, tinny music. Amongst them was a ten year old boy named Tom who was accompanied by his Mother Maggie. The music grew louder as they approached the colossal tent; beside himself with joy, Tom ran ahead of his Mother through the open archway and ran to the front to bagsy a couple of prime seats on the front row. Maggie soon caught up with him, breathless and giggling herself.

'Oh we'll have a great crack Tom; I only wish your Father was here too, but it serves him right for

getting mouldy drunk last night and twisting his owl ankle!'

On the other side of the circus ring at the back of the tent there was a gap in the folds and Tom could see lights flickering there. He badly needed to know what they were; and as he desperately needed to pee too he had the perfect excuse to slip out. His Mother cautioned him to be quick as it was cold and dark out there and the show was sure to start soon. Tom skirted the edge of the ring and slipped through the rear exit, only to discover nothing but darkness out there with not a flickering light in sight. Disappointed as he was, the urge to pee had become a hot pain in his groin so he made his way over to a tree. When he'd finished he turned to go back in the tent when his peripheral vision was alerted to a glow coming from the side of a wagon to his left.

Tom walked towards the light and as he reached the wagon something jumped out at him, giving him the fright of his life; it was a dwarf dressed as Leprechaun! The dwarf was doing a jig whilst holding three small fiery clubs close to his chest. The flames illuminated the little man's wizened old face, his black eyes shone with malice, and his lipless grin held no warmth, his orange curly wig, visible beneath his emerald green top hat, appeared to be crisping and receding beneath the brim from the intense heat of the clubs. The dwarf began to laugh then, scaring Tom so terribly, the urgent need to pee again hit him instantly.

The dwarf began to juggle the clubs and something strange happened, an image appeared in the ring of fire, Tom couldn't quite make it out, but he knew it was wondrous, it started to move away from him, desperate to see it clearly, to possess it, he followed, reaching out his hand trying to grasp it, needing to pull it into his soul; and just as he was close to reaching it, to consuming it, his feet fell from under him and he felt himself fall into darkness. Head over heels, head over heels grasping at air he fell until he finally came to land hard in a mud bath.

Tom's eyes adjusted quickly to his

surroundings and he could see he was in a forest. He looked back over his shoulder and could dimly make out the steep embankment he had fallen over. He got to his feet, relieved that he didn't seem to have broken any bones, and tried to climb back up. He could still hear the circus music, though it seemed impossibly far away. Try as he might he could not make any headway as the embankment was like a mudslide and he just kept slipping back down into the mud bath. Caked in filth, shivering uncontrollably with fear and bone penetrating cold, he wanted his Mother urgently, but knew if he stayed where he was he would not survive the night.

Feeling ahead of himself with outstretched arms he began to take tentative steps, and after progressing about a hundred yards without mishap he grew in confidence and picked up his pace somewhat; though he then became a little too cocky and walked face first into a tree. His poor nose took the brunt of the impact, his eyes smarted with shock and pain; and a warm fluid trickled from the injured member over his lips and chin. Tom had had enough, he collapsed to the ground in a heap and began to sob deeply with his bloody chin sagged onto his chest.

'Ah, what's all the hollerin about, for the love of Jesus would you ever stop wailing like a baby?'

Tom looked up to see the face of a boy irradiated by the glow of an old fashioned oil lamp he was holding up high.

'Michael Declan O'Dare's me name and rescuing Gobshites is me game! Come on so, and I'll get you out of here'.

Tom could see that the boy was around his own age, height and build, but had an unruly mass of red curls, a pale face full of freckles and warm green eyes. He wore no coat, just a puffed sleeve shirt, with knee length shorts, long socks and beat up old boots. Tom got to his feet and began to follow his saviour.

'Me names Tom, tanks very much Michael, I've never been so glad to see someone in all me life; but what are you doing yourself walking around the forest at night on your own?'

'You can call me Micky, I was lost meself a while back, and prayed for somebody to find me, so now I hang around whenever I can to light the way for other lost kids'.

'Do you live with the circus people Micky, who saved you when you were lost?'

The pale boy gazed off into the distance forlornly:

'I went to a circus once, but no Tom, I'm from the village, same as you, I've just been gone a while is all', then he returned from his reverie:

'You ask an awful lot of questions, so here's one for yourself, would you ever give your owl tongue a rest?'

He then set off walking again and began to whistle good naturedly. Tom followed his lead full of admiration for this fearless boy, but also feeling a strange sense of pity for him without knowing why. They'd walked for maybe ten minutes, zig zagging their way through the dense undergrowth and trees, when Micky came to an abrupt stop, raising the lamp *high, he pointed and said:*

'Follow that path there, it will take you out to the front of the circus tent, go straight into your Mother, and look after yourself, goodbye now and good luck'.

'Tanks Micky, but where are you going, can't you come with me and me Ma will take you home?'

'No I can't Tom, but you could do me a good turn if you've a mind to? Would you knock on the door of me Mammy's house, Mary O'Dare is her name; and tell her I love her and miss her homemade soda bread awful bad, she used to give me thick slices of it straight from the oven covered with melted butter; tell her that I'm OK and close by, I just can't come home yet', then he turned away.

Feeling terribly uneasy, Tom looked over his shoulder down the path, he quickly looked back to plead with Micky to change his mind, but he was gone.

Tom ran up the length of the path, and sure enough, at the end of it was the circus tent, and there at the entrance was his dear Mother talking to Constable Quinn:

'Mammy, oh Mammy!' he yelled as he ran to her.

'Oh Tom son, where have you been, are you alright, I've been so worried; and look at the state of you, what happened to your face son?'

'Of Mammy I followed a Leprechaun and fell down a hill and I was lost and walked into a tree and then a boy came along called Michael Declan O'Dare who wasn't afraid of anything, and he saved me Mammy, but he wouldn't come back with me and I don't know where he is!', he babbled.

The blood drained from his Mother's face, she exchanged an anxious look with Constable Quinn:

'Tom my poor boy did you knock your head when you fell son? Michael Declan O'Dare was a boy I went to school with over twenty years ago, but he disappeared when the circus came to town when he was only ten years old; and he's never been seen since then, but he would be the same age as me now son?'

Tom paled himself and shivered.

'Alright so Mammy, would you take me to see Mary O'Dare please, for I have a message for her from her poor lost boy.......

When we weren't being scared by Teresa's ghost stories we had plenty to do in the neighbourhood. A few streets up from ours there was an adventure playground that took up half of one side of the street. It had a ramshackle fence made up of odds and ends of boards and old doors. There were makeshift climbing frames, a pulley on a long thick rope and swings fashioned from decaying car tyres. It was staffed by a great group of young Men and Women who we referred to as the Hippies. They'd do all kinds of activities with us, arts, crafts, games, trips out to local parks etc.; and they were always kind, cheerful and endlessly patient with us allegedly underprivileged kids.

In summer they would make us chilled

homemade lemonade, in winter they'd give us big, frothy mugs of hot chocolate. The adventure playground was open all spring and summer during school holidays and weekends, but in winter I believe they only opened about one weekend a month, and for special events such as Halloween, Bonfire Night and Christmas week when they'd organize great parties for us.

There was a piece of wasteland across from the adventure playground that the Hippies used to build a huge bonfire on one particularly memorable Bonfire night. The evening started well as Mammy wrapped Tommy and I up in warm coats, scarves and gloves; and gave us packets of sparklers and bags of treacle toffee to take with us. Daddy took us to the Bonfire, on the way up the road, Tommy and I giggled and skipped, barely able to contain our excitement. However, as we approached the end of the street we saw crowds of people standing around the fire, silently staring into the flames.

As we got closer we could see the horrified expressions in their eyes. There was an overwhelmingly pungent odour in the air; the only thing I could compare it to is the smell of burning rubber and singed, meat, it filled my nostrils and I could actually taste it on my tongue, making me gag involuntarily. Daddy asked a man he knew what was going on. The man told him that a gang of teenagers had thrown a poor little dog deep into the fire earlier when it had been left unattended for just a few minutes; the boys had been seen running away laughing. The man only lived a few doors up and had heard the terrified agonized yelps from the creature as it was trapped in the fire, burning alive. The man ran to the scene within moments and reached it the same time as the Hippies. They all tried to get the dog out using sticks and bare hands, they managed to, but it was too late, the poor thing had died. Tommy and I burst into tears which set off the other children wailing too, we were inconsolable, so Daddy took us back home. I had the most awful nightmares about that little dog for months afterwards; and I've never forgotten that truly dreadful smell.

One night soon afterwards when my parents went out for the evening and Teresa was babysitting us we heard a faint rumble from above which was enough to spur Teresa into almost hysterical action.

'Momma, ah Momma, it's tunder and lightening! It'll burn the house down, we're gonna be roasted alive! Come on we have to get out of here!

Her face was flushed a hot pink, perspiration had broken out above her upper lip. She grabbed Shirley from her pram and bundled Tommy and I out of the front door and began to knock hysterically on our neighbour Margaret's door:

'Margaret, Margaret, open the door in the honour of God let me in!'

As an alarmed Margaret opened her door Teresa barged passed her with us in tow.

'Jesus save us, where's the fire?' asked a bewildered Margaret of Teresa's retreating back.

Teresa was actually crying by this stage and beyond any attempts of reasoning with her. She babbled barely coherent about lightening, and fires and burning. I could see that Margaret was dying to laugh, but didn't want to inflame the situation.

'Margaret have you got an owl (old) blanket I could borrow, but it has to be a big yoke (thing) please?' asked a shaking Teresa.

Margaret duly produced a big colourful blanket, which Teresa took from her. She draped one end over the back of Margaret's couch, and the other end over the dining table situated a few feet away.

'Tanks Margaret, now if I could just trouble you for a cushion I'll be on me way?'

Margaret handed her the cushion:

'On your way where Teresa?'

'To hide under the blanket 'til the tunder and lightening has gone; and I'm not coming out unless your house starts to burn down!' And with that she crawled into her hidey hole leaving poor Margaret to take care of us.

A little while later Margaret gave Tommy and me some orange juice. Shirley was sleeping soundly on the couch:

'Margaret I'm going to see Teresa now, would it be OK for me to take my drink with me to share with her?' I asked.

Margaret laughed.

'Of course darlin', and I'll go and get one for crazy too!' she replied kindly.

I crawled under the blanket to join crazy, though I could tell that she didn't want to talk as she was holding on fiercely to a set of Rosary beads and mumbling Hail Mary prayers with her eyes squeezed shut. So I just sat on the floor with her, believing my comforting presence would help. A hand appeared in the semi-darkness holding a glass of orange juice, which I placed on the floor for Teresa, but she didn't even open her eyes. Eventually the storm passed, and all became still and quiet apart from the gentle hum of the television in the background. I was stiffening up in the awkward position I was sitting in:

'Come on Teresa, the tunder and lightening is finished will we go home now?'

But she refused to budge until Margaret went next door to our house to check it hadn't burned to the ground. When Margaret gave the all clear, we went back home. Teresa blessed her face before we passed back through our front door:

'Blessed God I know I'm a lurkey fool, but tanks very much for not letting the house burn down to the ground, and now I know you're looking after us I won't panic agin. Amen'.

However, she soon forgot her promise to

God, and every time thereafter that there was even the slightest tremorin the air, lurkey would lose the plot again!

Chapter 11

The Guilt Trip

These days there is much research and evidence available which demonstrates the detrimental impact of domestic abuse on the psychological and emotional development of children; though, during the 1960s and 1970s even if there was some awareness of the issue very little was done about it.

It was about a year after I started school that the emotional abuse at home began to take its physical toll on me. It started with the headaches. They would build slowly early afternoons in class, but by home time my eyes would be watering, I would feel nauseous; and the pain in my head was so bad I was sure my brain would explode. When Mammy came to collect Tommy and me from school I would be a pale and trembling wreck, though I wouldn't cry, I didn't want the other children to see my weakness, but as soon as I got through the door at home I would scream and cry and throw myself on the settee covering my head with my hands in agony, the screaming only made it worse. Mammy would try to help by giving me aspirin, but it didn't touch the pain, which was excruciating.

After two days of this my Mother took me to the doctor's. He diagnosed childhood migraine and gave her a prescription for me. I remember looking at him through blurred vision and seeing an expression of pity in his eyes. He'd treated Mammy on many occasions after Daddy's beatings; and he told her that there was no doubt in his mind that I was deeply disturbed by the violence at home. My Mother lowered her head, clearly feeling guilt about the affects witnessing domestic violence had on her child, but knowing that she had very little control in bringing about positive change. The medication the doctor gave me helped with the headaches, but then I began to exhibit other physical signs of a troubled mind.

Firstly I began to squeeze my eyes shut just for a second every few minutes. This was closely followed a few weeks later by me pulling my upper lip into my mouth which provided a most satisfying feeling of stretching my nose. Finally I would jerk both my shoulders upwards. Anybody sitting next to me must have found the experience intolerably irritating for it must have appeared to others that I had choreographed my routine much as a dancer or gymnast would, that I had some control over the behaviour, but it was entirely involuntary; squeeze eyes, stretch nose, jump, squeeze eyes, stretch nose, jump, squeeze eyes, stretch nose, jump.

This went on continuously for months during all my waking hours. I'm sure nobody wanted to sit next to me in class, but had no choice and the teacher eventually gave up on telling me to stop fidgeting. The behaviour just became a part of me and I was almost oblivious to these annoying habits.

The same could not be said of those around me. Teresa refused to be in the same room as me except for bedtimes (asleep I was still as a log). Mammy seemed to pass no heed, probably thinking that it would go away if she didn't make a big deal of it. Daddy, on the other hand, evidently had an awareness of the root of the problem and didn't feel easy about it.

One evening I was sitting beside him on the gold vinyl settee watching the TV. I don't recall what we were watching, though I remember being engrossed in the programme, and unaware as usual of my ticks, stretches, and jumps when all of a sudden my Father jumped to his feet and started yelling at me at the top of his voice:

'Stop, Jesus Christ in the name of God will you stop fucking jumping and blinking!'

I froze. Mammy came into the living room from the kitchen:

'Tommy what are you roaring for? What's going on?'

Then she saw the crestfallen expression on my face. I began to shake, tears poured from my eyes. I tried to tell Daddy that I was sorry, that I would try to stop being a nuisance; but the words only stammered on my petrified lips. Daddy saw the fear in my eyes too, and swept me up in his arms, he held me tight against his chest, his own wracked with sobs, he said:

'Don't cry baby, I'm so, so sorry', over and over again.

Eventually we all calmed down just as Teresa came bouncing through the front door. My Father told her we were going on a little trip. I wrapped up in my heavy winter coat, woolly hat, scarf and gloves; and held my Father's hand as we walked down the cold, dark street like nothing had happened at all. My legs and face stung from the icy blasts of bitter winds.

Daddy took me and Teresa to the local shop and gave the man behind the counter ten bob and told him to give us whatever we wanted. The contrast of the warmth of the shop made me go all tingly. We knew the shop keeper well; he was a kind, good humoured man. His face lit up as he waved his arm dramatically across the many rows of shelves of multi-coloured jars of sweets, showing his wares as though he were a magician performing a great act of magic.

There's a reason why that song proclaims that a spoonful of sugar helps the medicine go down; filling a binbag with sweets, pop and crisps helped me forget the trauma of that day, at least for a while.

Although it was a short therapeutic excursion for me; it was a long guilt trip that my

Father embarked on that day, a journey that I don't believe he ever stopped travelling.

Chapter 12

The Boy

As a child I grew up knowing all about my Mother's background, but knew very little of my Father's history. It was only as a young adult that I began to learn about his deeply disturbed upbringing. He grew up in Ireland. His Mother, Mago, in Daddy's memories of her was a saint who died at the age of forty-six after a life filled with suffering. His memories of his Father Thomas were very different. Daddy would grind his teeth whenever he talked of Thomas, he would call him as an evil bastard whom he had no love or fondness for at all.

Out of earshot of my Father Mammy told me that even amongst travellers who widely accepted that domestic violence and other forms of abuse of women was part of married life, my

Grandfather Thomas Doherty was often referred to as an animal by traveller women and men alike. Mammy's Mother, Ellie had told her tales of Mago's screams echoing all around the campsites when Thomas beat her; he was known as a biter, which accounted for the spine tingling screams.

When he was four years old, along with his two sisters, my Father was removed from his parent's care. Daddy never knew the full circumstances surrounding this event, though he always clearly recalled the day it happened. He was taken by people from the local authority in a big black car with his older sister Mary Margaret who was aged five at the time. After a long journey the car stopped and he was taken out. The car drove on and he and Mary Margaret waved goodbye to each other through the window; neither of them aware then that they would be fully grown before they would meet again.

I have in my possession an admissions form for the children's home he was sent to which simply referred to him as:

The boy, 4 years old, Father an itinerant with no visible means of supporting his family.

I've since learned that it was quite common place in Ireland in those days for children to be put in the care of the local authority for such reasons. His sisters went to other children's homes; he had no contact with his siblings in all the years he remained in care until his brother Johnny joined him in the home when my Father was aged about thirteen.

Daddy had one, only one, pleasant memory of being in care. When he was aged five he developed an abscess on his leg which made him very ill, one of the nuns from the nearby convent nursed him back to health and was kind and affectionate to him. This was the singular act of kindness he experienced there.

Daddy occasionally talked of the cruelty

inflicted upon the children in the home by the Brothers (the Priests) and the local farmers who they were made to work for free of charge. The children were virtually starved and regularly beaten, and were worked like dogs. Though my Father never discussed the sexual abuse of the boys by the Priests in the home; Uncle Johnny has since told me it was systematic and rife. Boys would be taken from their beds in the middle of the night to darker places by the Priests who God was supposed to have sent to Earth to protect them.

Traumatized by their ordeals, many wet their beds, and would be beaten and humiliated in the presence of the other boys, often made to sleep in their soiled bedding for many a night for their acts of ungodliness. The boys were given some schooling, although this was probably a funding requirement by the local authority. The hours in the classroom were few compared to those spent grafting in the home and fields.

Daddy had been there possibly two or three years when Mago and Thomas paid him a visit. The visit took place in a small room with a window set high up in the wall. He had been in the room on other occasions to clean it so was familiar with the layout. He asked his Mother to lift him up so he could see out of the window because he had always wanted to know what was on the other side. He never recalled what he saw when she raised him up, only how wonderful it felt to have Mago's arms around him again. He begged her to take him with her when she was leaving, she cried and appeared heartbroken when she told him she couldn't, and then she was gone. His parents never visited him again.

When he was around sixteen years of age my Father was sent into the Town to learn a trade with a local tailor. He stayed there just long enough to learn the basic skills of cutting and sewing. He then took off to join the Army, as you had to be seventeen to sign up he lied about his age. Whilst a member of the Army he brushed up on his skills in tailoring and became a boxer. Daddy had a lot of anger in him so quickly gained a reputation as a tough fighter, a real contender for professional boxing one day.

After a year he took some leave to track down his Mother. He found her living with Thomas in a small Town. Mago was delighted to see her first born Son who'd now grown into a handsome man resembling a young Frank Sinatra; she showered him with hugs and kisses. It wasn't long before Thomas turned dog with Mago, starting an argument with her for no reason, he then picked up an old flat iron, raised it above his head, and went to strike her with it. However, Daddy, anticipating Thomas's intention was already moving toward him; he leaped across the kitchen floor and throwing himself between his parents he grabbed his Father's wrist in a vice like grip.

Thomas saw the hatred and defiance in his son's eyes, defeated; he lowered his arm with a sunken head. Mago wept, turned to her drunken, violent Husband and said:

'There now, you bad bastard, my Tommy is here and he'll never let you hurt me again!'

My Father returned to the Army barracks the next day. About a week later he was summoned to the office to be brought before the sergeant where he was given his discharge papers. Thomas had contacted the Police who in turn notified the Army that his son was underage when he joined . He was devastated, with no idea of what his future would hold and his family scattered all over England and Ireland; he made the decision to take the few pounds he had in his pocket and get the boat to England in search of his sister Mary Margaret who he'd heard was working in a Woolworth's store in London.

After a long journey by bus, ferry and

coach my Father arrived in London on a lovely summer's day. He headed straight for Woolworths, walking through the main door into the enormous confectionery section; he approached the counter and asked the young woman serving if Mary Margaret still worked there. The assistant told him that she did indeed and went off to fetch her. He didn't have to wait long. He hadn't seen his sister for thirteen years, and now it was a beautiful young woman who approached him:

'You're Tommy aren't you?' she stated, for it wasn't really a question.

He cried as he replied that it was him, and they both sobbed as they embraced tightly. That was one of my Father's happiest memories, and he retold the tale often throughout his life. He always adored Aunt Margaret, he loved all his siblings, but she was his favourite, he even named his oldest daughter after her.

Margaret moved to the USA in the late

1960s or early 1970s, but they remained close despite the distance, via letters and phone. If the Irish Government couldn't keep them apart forever, the Atlantic Ocean had no chance!

Chapter 13

Disappearing World

My Father settled in Birmingham for a couple of years earning a living collecting and weighing scrap and tarmacking whilst staying in digs. When he was aged 19 he moved to Manchester where he met my Mother. She was only 15 years old at the time, but he always said that it was love at first sight for him, and he knew that one day he would marry her. However, there was a bit of an obstacle in the form of another young traveller man by the name of Michael who Mammy had an understanding with that she would marry him.

Not to be put off by such a trifling problem Daddy kept close enough for her to keep him in mind whilst still allowing her time to grow up some more and then set about wooing her. They married when she was 18 and he was 22, though we still have my Mother's wedding dress there are no photos of the special day because Uncle Johnny who was then living in Manchester too, went off to the park with his new girlfriend, and, the all-important camera.

My parents moved to Birmingham soon after where I was born on May 28th 1963. Even though Daddy was working they didn't have much and I had to sleep in a drawer for the first few months on my life. They returned to Manchester just before my Brother Tommy was born on September 17th 1964, as my Mother was missing her family and work was plentiful here at that time.

We had been settled in Criccieth Street for a good few years when Uncle Charlie came over from Ireland to visit us. For the many years that my Father had been in the children's home he hadn't known that he had two younger Brothers, Charlie and Simey. When he learned of their existence he had returned to Ireland a few years before to meet them.

Charlie must have been aged 16 when I first saw him. He was small, slim and wearing a denim jacket and jeans. He'd coloured his wavy hair auburn and looked like the American actor Audey Murphy, he was so handsome. Teresa would have been aged 13, and the two of them had an instant attraction to each other. I knew Teresa liked him because she was initially uncharacteristically shy, avoiding his inspection she averted her gaze and stared at the floor. Though the sheepishness didn't last long before her true colours came through when she began to poke fun at his height and strong Irish accent. Charlie had a big hearty laugh and responded good naturedly to her teasing.

I watched the two of them flirting with each other all evening. I didn't know it was flirting at the time, though I did know that the banter between them was harmless, fun to watch and that they clearly enjoyed each other's company.

    Later that evening my parents headed off to the pub as usual, leaving Teresa and Charlie to babysit me, Tommy and Shirley. Teresa settled the two younger ones in bed and left me to chaperone the evening between herself and her new admirer. We put the telly on, Teresa and I were comfy on the settee, and Charlie was a safe, chaste distance away in an armchair. A programme came on called Disappearing World which provided insights into the lives of remote African tribes, and other cultures, not the type of programme ordinarily of interest to most teenagers one would assume. However, from initially paying scant attention, their eyes soon became riveted to the screen when a band of women began to perform a traditional African tribal dance. The dance was undoubtedly a lovely spectacle to behold, but the reason those two were so engrossed was because the dusky beauties were dancing topless, their bare breasts bounced all over the place in perfect time to the rhythm of the ferocious drumbeats. Charlie and Teresa sat in stunned silence, both purple faced with embarrassment. I felt ashamed of my life myself for watching what all good Catholics would surely deem a dirty programme, then my nerves got the better of me and I burst out laughing. They looked at me, clearly shocked at my waywardness, then looked at each other and started howling with laughter themselves.

'Kate and Tommy would go stone mad if they knew we were watching that yoke, turn it off Mary quick!' demanded Teresa.

Then with a mischievous twinkle in her eye she said:

'I've got a great idea I'll be back in a minute!'

She quickly returned with Daddy's air rifle and beckoned us with her hand to follow her as she crept up the stairs and into my parent's front bedroom. Leaving the light off she approached the big sash window, moved the white net curtain aside, and pushed upwards to open the window a couple of inches. Crouching down she placed the nozzle of the rifle through the opening, camouflaged herself a little with the net, then in the manner of an expert marks man without hesitation she pulled the trigger. A Smokey smell assaulted my nostrils and my heart leaped into my stomach.

'There now, that crabby bitch across the street has a hole in her winda and the next time tells me to go on about my business again I'll know it was me what did it!' she declared triumphantly.

Charlie and I just giggled nervously, for though it was very risky, it was great fun, an adventure. A few minutes later she spotted a young man staggering up the street, evidently the worse for drink:

'Oh Momma, look at your man? I'm

gonna give him the surprise of his life!'

As the man passed by the opposite side of the street she took aim and fired.

The poor man leaped into the air; startled into sobriety he began slapping his backside repeatedly whilst yelling:

'Jesus Christ what the fuck was that?'

He looked desperately about him, though his horrified eyes saw nothing obvious, and rubbing the injured area, he quickly moved on.

Charlie and Teresa were so convulsed with laughter they couldn't breathe. However, I thought she'd gone a step too far, I was aghast:

'Teresa, in the honour of God what were you tinking? You just shot the poor man in the arse, me Mammy and Daddy will kill us if they find out!'

This remonstration didn't have the desired effect I'd hoped for, it just made them worse, and they rolled about the floor holding their bellies which were cramped with laughter pain.

The next morning Charlie left early to go out working with Daddy for the day. When they returned that evening an altercation took place between them. I can't recall what it was about, though I'll never forget the expression of sadness upon Charlie's handsome face when Daddy slapped him across it and made his nose bleed. He left our house immediately after despite my Mother's assurances that my Father was sorry, he wouldn't do it again and pleas for him to stay.

I didn't see my Uncle Charlie again for about nine years when he visited us in our Fallowfield home with his young wife and two year old Son Louis. The carefree boy with the easy laugh and auburn hair was gone; in his place was a man of responsibilities who would be plagued by mental health problems for the rest of his troubled life. The World Charlie had once known had truly disappeared.

Chapter 14

Petty Crimes And Punishment

Auntie Eileen, also known as Daughter, had two daughters of her own, Caren and Sandra who were very close to us. We saw them on a daily basis as they lived around the corner from our house, and were of a similar age to Tommy and me. So one evening when I called at their house with my Mother, and popped my head around their bedroom door I was surprised to see them both snuggled up in bed drinking tea from baby's bottles. They went purple with shame when I burst out laughing.

They went everywhere with us, wherever Daddy had a notion to take us. Parks, Museums, country walks, Belle Vue, an amusement park on Hyde Road Manchester, that first opened its doors in the 1870s and was once advertised as the showground of the World, which finally closed it's adventurous doors in 1980. Of course all this fun and frivolity came with a price; after all you have to take the rough with the smooth! Consequently, if Sandra and Caren were found guilty of crimes and misdemeanours with Tommy and me they would be punished equally.

We were raised the old fashioned way with certain behaviours expected of us. Never interrupt adults when they are talking, do as you were told and don't answer back etc. If any of us broke these implicitly holier than thou rules, punishment was metered out promptly; and in our childish views, somewhat harshly.

My Father would assess the severity of the crime before passing sentence. An answer back might warrant grounding for one day. Losing money would mean no sweets for at least a few days. However, serious breaches in behavioural etiquette would require the quick production of the clothes brush. This particular instrument of torture was only brought out in the most severe cases, for example, not returning home at the appointed time or breaking an ornament as a result of careless shenanigans.

Daddy would make all four of us line up side by side with one hand behind our backs and the other stretched out in front of us. The extended guilty limbs would be trembling as we stared at the clothes brush with its menacing long, flat handle which was about eight inches in length by two inches in width and was as robust and sturdy as the man holding it by its soft bristly harmless part.

My Father considered himself a fair man and I'm sure he took no pleasure in the task, though likewise, I don't believe he was disturbed by it in the least either. His motto was if you can't do the time don't do the crime! We would each be given three short, sharp raps with the handle on our tender little palms. With eyes smarting, faces flushed and feeling very hard done by, all would then be forgiven by my Father. We could return to our adventures with a clean slate and a slight resentment at the injustice of it all; though this would soon be forgotten until the next transgression, which was never long in my case.

I have always been fiercely protective of my siblings; nevertheless, on one particularly memorable occasion I took my responsibilities a little too far. There was a boy who lived on the corner of our street who was forever teasing and tormenting Tommy.

One meltingly hot summer's day when the temperature were so high the tarmac covering the road was bubbling in parts, and giving off an shimmering haze; Tommy and I were playing in the street with a group of other kids including the bully boy. Who for no perceivable reason gave Tommy a resounding thump into the side of his head?

Tommy crashed to the floor too shocked from the unexpected blow to even cry. My face already flushed from the intense heat burned with anger. Without hesitation I looked around me for something to hurt the boy with; and spotted my weapon of retaliation instantly, a piece of rubber hose a couple of yards long and a good inch thick. I reached down for it where it lay discarded in the gutter, grabbed it, ran at the villain and began to whip him around his legs and torso without mercy. I was so consumed with rage I don't know if I would have stopped if it wasn't for the sound of a woman's terrified screams:

'Oh my Son, my poor boy, stop that you little bitch!'

It was the boy's Mother she was enraged and grabbing my arm roughly she tore the hose from my hand, casting it aside she dragged me by my arm and her injured child by his to my front door. Her son was wailing inconsolably.

Mammy appeared in response to the hammering at the door. The woman began yelling at my Mother telling her that I was an evil little bitch, that I'd nearly killed her Angel stone dead. The Angel wailed louder, then to add weight to her claims he swooned and sagged to the floor whilst his righteously indignant Mother watched in horror.

Mammy was clearly mortified, with a face wrought crimson by humiliation she yanked me by my arm through the door and smacked me hard tree times on my bottom. The injured Angel stopped his wailing and swooning and grinned at me slyly beneath his sweaty, tousled mop of hair. My Mother rarely hit me, but the sting of her disapproval hurt me far more than my smarting bottom. Shoving me roughly down the hall she yelled:

'You get up those stairs to your room right now, and just you wait 'til your Father gets home! And as for you, I will make sure my child is punished for what she did to yours, but don't you ever call her a bitch again!'

Her words hung heavy in the air, landing cumbersomely on my shoulders as I walked on leaden legs up the stairs to my room. The hours until Daddy returned home from work stretched out endlessly, but eventually I heard him coming through the front door, his arrival signalled by the customary clearing of his throat. He'd barely put his foot in the hall before I heard Mammy apprising him with the details of my abominable escapade.

'What Kate, Mary? Are you serious? I can't believe it! Where the hell is she?'

'She's in her room, but Tommy for God's sake calm down, don't go too far!' My Mother remonstrated.

Now that she'd told the tale as required by duty she was distraught by the fear of him punishing me too severely.

I was in an awful state of anxiety upstairs

sat up in bed, gripping handfuls of the pink candlewick bedspread in fists, heart hammering at my ribcage, blinking and jumping up a storm, my nerves in tatters. I heard Daddy stomping up the stairs at least two, possibly three at a time. The door few open crashing against the wall, and when I saw his face I knew instantly that punishment by clothes brush would have been a merciful sentence! My own Father looked like he was going to murder me! Then a miracle occurred, the fury disappeared from his countenance, instantly replaced by an expression of profound sadness. He sat beside me on the bed reached for my hand and said:

'It's alright baby, you've done a very bad ting, but don't be so afraid of me in the honour of God, I won't hurt you!'

I burst into overwhelmingly relieved tears. He hugged me then and made it all go away. My Mother had been standing in the doorway watching all the time; she would never have allowed him to go too far with any of her babies. She came over and kissed the top of my head whilst he was still holding me.

'What are we going to do with you, you bad girl?' she asked softly.

'I know I did a bad ting, but that boy is horrible. He hit Tommy and knocked him down, and I couldn't let him get away with that, could I!' They both ignored my defensive plea entirely though.

'Well she can't get away with it altogether. She'll have to stay in her room after school and all weekend for a whole week, no playing out, no television' Daddy declared.

I did too. It wasn't so bad though, as I was allowed to read, colour in books and draw to pass the time; and every day after work Daddy would join me to admire my creations and tell me about his day.

I learned a valuable lesson from the experience. That no matter what our expectations of others are; we are all capable of surprising each other with the decisions we make.

However, old habits die hard. A few years later I went on the war path again. A boy we knew well hit Tommy knocking him to the ground in the process, and true to form I picked up a weapon, that time it was a four by two plank of wood and walloped the boy across his arse with it. The boy fortunately for me, was the forgiving type. He didn't inform on me to our parents and bore me no malice for what he told me later he saw as a heroic act, one that led to him developing a huge crush on me. He certainly surprised me with the decision he made that day, and has remained a much valued lifelong friend of our family ever since.

Chapter 15

Give Me The Child Until He Is Seven

My Mother had a loving bond with her parents and siblings. Always the peacemaker and mediator she rarely had a cross word with any of them and was adored and looked up to by all of them. Her Father, Arthur was a lovely gentle soul who was educated to a degree and loved to read, an interest he shared with Daddy together with a similar sense of humour. They worked together collecting scrap and tarmacking for many years. Grandad Arthur never intervened in in my Mother and Father's relationship problems to my knowledge, though I find it unlikely that he didn't on some occasions at least, pass comment even in a non-threatening manner, to my Father on the many black eyes and swollen lips his beloved daughter

Kate sustained at the brutal hands of his Son- In-Law.

He himself was all too familiar with domestic abuse at the hands of his wife, my Nanna Ellie, the matriarch of the family. Grandad liked a few pints, but never to excess, though he was awful fond of his Park Drive cigarettes. A habit which was to be his downfall as he suffered from breathing difficulties, and was bed ridden the last few years of his life.

By that time he had moved to a new build flat in a high rise block with Nanna and Teresa near to their old rented house that had been demolished. My enduring memories of him are of him lying in his bed propped up by a mound of pillows, with a stack of paperback books, numerous asthma inhalers, pills and potions, cigarettes and matches covering his bedside cabinet.

I would occasionally stay overnight at the flat with Teresa, and we would go into his room to pass the time for him and listen to his stories of Ireland and of his first experiences of living in England. We never stayed with him too long as he tired easily and slept a lot.

Teresa and I would get in the double bed she shared with Nanna and wait for her to come back from the pub, hoping she would be in good humour. When she was she would join us in the bed, we'd be at the bottom, she'd be at the top, with a sup of tea beside her and would smoke a few Park Drives whilst telling us who'd been in the pub and how the night had gone. She had very long hard toenails which would scrape our legs all night long as she tossed and turned in her fitful sleep, we would just endure the discomfort for it wasn't wise to cross Nanna.

When she came home in a darker mood we would have to pull the eiderdown over our heads to try to dull the sounds of her tormenting poor Grandad with her vitriolic streams of verbal abuse yelled through the wall to him from the comfort of her bed. Grandad rarely retaliated, if he did in the form of a weak plea:

'Ellie, please in the honour of God will you stop!'

It only made matters worse, and her cruel taunts would reach new heights. They had once been happy, certainly in the first few years of their marriage when they'd lived a simple country life raising their family in Kerry, a picturesque, quaint small Town in Southern Ireland. Together they had nine children, only seven of whom survived to adulthood. Two died before the age of three, the first Mary Teresa and Patrick were taken by diseases which were common causes of death in children in those days. The surviving children were Thomas (Son) their first born, followed by Eileen (Daughter), then Kate, Michael, Arthur, Jim, and lastly, Mary Teresa the second (Teresa).

Not long after Arthur was born Nanna became very ill with septicaemia and almost died. Due to her illness and long recovery period Uncle Arthur was sent to live with Nanna's Mother, Mainee. It's very common practice in traveller families for the Grandparents to rear one or more of their Son or Daughter's children; and Arthur remained with Mainee even though Ellie had long recovered and subsequently had two more children.

A few years later when Son was aged around seventeen he came to England to seek his fortune. Nanna and Grandad took their other children and followed him over, leaving Arthur behind with Mainee. My Mother was fifteen years old when she left the emerald Isle and never lived there again, although she returned on many occasions over the years to attend the annual horse racing event at Ballybunion, but mostly to attend family funerals. England became her home and she loved it.

Son settled down with an English girl with whom he had five children. He later married a traveller woman with whom he had four more children. He was serving a four year prison sentence at the time for assaulting a police officer, a crime he did not actually commit it had been a case of mistaken identity. The real perpetrator had lost the coin from a gold sovereign ring at the scene of the crime and matched Son's description, and as Son had a different coin in his ring from the original one, but couldn't prove that he had replaced it years before, as a traveller and known to the police, he was a perfect fit for being set up for the offense.

Daughter married a man from Belfast and had five children with him. Michael also settled with an English girl and had two children with her. Jim always kept Nanna's home as his base, until he was in his forties when he finally settled down, he married a traveller woman with whom he had one daughter.

Teresa married an English man named Alan, they had four children together. Their only

Son, Lee died tragically in an accident in a lift when he was aged eleven, a loss they have never recovered from. My Mother married my Father when he won the hand of the fair Lady having stolen her from under the nose of his fierce rival, Michael, when she was aged eighteen and Daddy was aged twenty-two.

When my parents returned to Manchester they rented a two up two down terraced house on Demark Road, Moss Side. One year and three months after my birth my Brother Tommy was born in St Mary's hospital on September 17th 1964. Mammy was still convalescing in hospital after her second traumatic delivery when Daddy turned up at visiting time with a young man she didn't initially recognise for it had been many years since she had last seen him. It was her Brother Arthur. She told me often of this meeting. Arthur had turned up at our house earlier that day looking for his Sister Kate, and my Father took him to see her at the hospital.

Mammy described her first sighting of him as incredibly moving. She said he was shy and stood awkwardly, and was beautiful, just like a film star. Standing over six feet tall with broad shoulders, high cheekbones, full lips and a shock of wavy dark blonde hair which was well oiled and worn in a duck tail fashion. He sat beside her on the edge of the bed and placed his arms around her shoulders, they held each other tightly and both wept. From that moment onwards she loved him just as much as her other siblings.

Things were not quite the same for Arthur. Though he settled in Manchester himself and later married his cousin Winnie with whom he had six children he only really had a bond with my Mother. He didn't feel, or wouldn't allow himself to feel, a connection with his other siblings. Arthur was interesting, funny and entertaining company, but in drink all his anger and bitterness would come out to play.

Because he had been raised by Mainie and not by his parents with his siblings, he always felt alienated. He never forgave Ellie for not taking him back when she recovered from her illness, and had no respect or real love for her, though he bore Grandad no malice as he was clearly not the decision maker. Being left behind when his own family moved to England and the ensuing sense of rejection was a lifelong source of pain and conflict for him.

All of the brothers and sisters were heavy drinkers, though in the heyday of the swinging sixties this wasn't really frowned upon at least not in our circles, but it was Uncle Arthur and Michael who became alcoholics, both died prematurely from alcohol related conditions, Arthur at aged forty two and Michael aged sixty.

One night my parents returned home from their usual pub crawl, it was late and Tommy, Shirley and I were tucked up in our beds. The commotion of them coming through the door roused me from my deep slumbers. A woman's terrified voice was crying out:

'He's gonna kill me!'

I leaped from my bed and ran to my now customary look out post at the top of the stairs with Tommy who'd also had a rude awakening. We looked down to see a pale, shaking and clearly horrified Winnie standing in the hallway. She was weeping and wringing her hands, my Mother was trying to calm her:

'He won't Winnie I won't let him near you I promise!'

But then the front door nearly came off its hinges with the force of the blows inflicted upon it.

'Give her out, give her out to me right fucking now yee fucking bastards!'

It was Uncle Arthur and he was angry as a bear snared in a net.

My heart leaped down into my stomach with an all-consuming sense of foreboding.

Mammy pushed poor Winnie towards the stairs:

'Get up the stairs quick mog, lock yourself in my room hurry up!'

The door crashed open and slammed against the wall. Arthur bolted through when Winnie was still only half way up the stairs. Daddy rushed towards Arthur, but Mammy was already trying to push him back out into the street. Daddy pulled her out of the way and took over the pushing himself though somewhat more gently as he simultaneously tried to placate Arthur. Pleading with him to calm down and think of what he was doing. Winnie stood beside us children reciting prayers over and over. By that stage Arthur was roaring and demanding that Daddy go outside to fight him; my Father was the voice of reason for once, Teresa and my Mother were screaming at Arthur whilst tearing at their own hair, Winnie was mumbling prayers, Tommy and I were whimpering; then all of a sudden Arthur yelled at the top of his voice:

'Alright, all fucking right will yee all shut up in the honour of God and fucking leave me alone!'

He backed out of the front door and slumped down onto the doorstep with shoulders drooped and head hung low; he was instantly deflated. Everyone watched in silence afraid that the beast would rise up again. But Arthur had no fight left in him; the beast was tamed, for the moment at least. He turned his head to the side and said:

'Winnie, come on, will we go home now?'

I turned to look at Winnie. The expression of relief on her face was palpable. She was a tall woman, but she went down those stairs with dainty steps without uttering a word. When she reached Arthur she gently tapped her Husband on his shoulder. He turned to look up at her, slowly rose to his feet, nodded in the general direction of the street; and off they went as if nothing had happened at all.

Arthur was a tormented soul, believing he was abandoned as a child he internalised a sense of shame and lack of importance all his life. He'd had a good life with Mainie and witnessed no alcohol and domestic abuse as had his siblings, but he always felt less worthy than them; and though he loved his wife and children dearly they paid a high price for the seed that was sown when he believed his own Mother deserted him all those years ago, and his anger made him a hard man to live with.

The tragedy is that none of them need have suffered in this way, for Nanna had returned for him before she set off for England, but Arthur was too young to remember Mainie pleading with Ellie to let him stay with her as Arthur clung to the hem of her dress refusing to leave her for his real Mother, how different might his life have been if he'd taken Ellie by the hand that day.

Chapter 16

A Tale Of Two Mothers

Nanna Ellie, Mammy's Mother, always looked far older than her years. Losing two children under the age of three, having two miscarriages, almost dying of septicaemia; and the subsequent many years of heavy drinking and smoking Park Drive cigarettes took their toll on her face. She also dressed like an elderly woman, head scarves, drab coats, American tan stockings, which she wore knotted at the back of her knees and dated dresses in the style of all the old traveller women of County Kerry. She could never be described as lovely or pretty though she had a lined, but handsome face with high cheekbones, a strong symmetrical jawline, full lips, soft brown hair that fell to her bottom, but was always worn scraped back from her face and wound into a tight bun at the nape of her neck; and clear green eyes that could assess the worth of the person their piercing gaze fell upon in seconds. Her perception of others was usually, but not always right, and if she didn't like somebody they knew about it instantly. She had a deep gravelly voice which she used to often devastating effect with tongue lashings that would emotionally floor the recipients.

When it came to her boys though, especially Son, she was putty in their hands. She had good relationships with Mammy and Daughter; however, she gave Teresa a very hard time. Teresa was the baby of the family and one would think she would have been cossetted and spoilt rotten by all, but she wasn't. She was cheeky and rebellious with a Devil may care attitude that didn't lend itself well to bringing out the best in others. Grandad Arthur was lovely and endlessly patient with her, conversely, Nanna had no time for Teresa's shenanigans, and regularly metered out harsh punishments to her wayward daughter. I recall one occasion when Teresa wrought the wrath of Ellie, though I don't recollect the details of the crime she was evidently guilty of. Teresa and I were playing outside her home, a large terraced house occupying a corner plot with a huge front garden just off Demark Road; when Nanna came out with a face purple with rage, snapped a thick branch of a tree in the garden, looked at Teresa and said:

'Gid in the house now you dirty brazen animal!'

I tremored with fear and pity for Teresa whom I loved dearly when I heard her screams escaping the open windows as Nanna beat her with the branch behind closed doors.

Whilst Grandad Arthur worked with Daddy in the Country Nanna did her part to support the family by travelling on foot or public transport to the nicer areas of Manchester.

She didn't refer to these outings as begging ventures, though essentially that's what they were. However, she felt no shame about it, after all a woman had to do what a woman had to do to help feed her family and fund her drinking habits. She took me along with her on a few of these enterprises. She would lead by example herself initially by instructing me to step back, watch, listen and learn. She would then knock on a door and when the lady of the house answered Nanna would adopt a Uriah Heap like posture and demeanour, she would actually ring her hands in a feigned demonstration of anxiety and say:

'Good morning misses how is yourself today? My poor Husband has passed away, God rest his blessed soul, leaving me to rear our ten childer all alone; please misses do you have any spare clothes or owl bits and bobs to help me and my hungry childer?'

People were generally kind and Nanna

seldom came away empty handed. Sometimes she'd ask me to do the talking and would give me a contrived tale to tell, we were always rewarded when I did the begging. One time a nice lady came out to us with a silver tray laden with a silver pot of tea, milk, sugar, buttered cream crackers and fancy biscuits. We sat on the curb in the warmth of the sunshine and tucked in.

At the end of the day Nanna would sell her somewhat ill-gotten gains to the second hand shops or the rag and bone men, and rewarded me for my labours too. After making a big pot of grub for the family she would then sit in her favourite armchair resplendent in her coat and headscarf waiting for the clock to strike seven then she'd head off to the pub.

During the early years of her marriage Nanna had rarely touched a drop of the demon brew except for a couple of Guinness at an infrequent wedding or funeral. But the tragedy of losing two toddlers and the miscarriages was more than she could bear. Consumed with despair, loss and bitterness she would drink herself into oblivion in whatever pub would serve her. There was not that many for in those times all pubs could legally display notices in their windows warning blacks and travellers that they were not permitted to enter the premises. The pubs in Ireland were even more discriminatory than the British ones; though Nanna never failed to find a funhouse in which to ride the carousal of inebriation each and every night.

Whist still in Ireland her poor kids would have to search the local town or village for her dragging a cart behind them until they found her and would put her insensible form onto the cart and take her home to Grandad who never uttered a word of recrimination to his troubled wife. The move to England provided Nanna with endless opportunities to try a different venue each night on her journey to forgetfulness. Nanna Ellie could be kind, thoughtful and generous when she chose to be to those in need; and often helped out less fortunate family members and neighbours with clothes, money and food. She was a formidable, complex woman and had she been educated she could have been anything she chose to be. Had she not suffered such great loss her children may have been raised in a stable environment; and there would have been no well-travelled path of alcohol and domestic abuse for them to follow her down.

I never met my Grandmother Mago, Daddy's Mother; she died of leukemia in Ireland aged forty-six June 1965. My Father always portrayed her as a saint and wouldn't have a bad word said about her. Her story is sketchy, but from what I've pieced together it seems that she had a horrendous life with her Husband Thomas. A hard, cold, violent man who showed her no mercy with the extreme beatings he subjected her to. Because of this and his itinerant and unemployed status at the time; Aunt Margaret aged 5, my Father aged 4 and Aunt Bridget aged 2 were removed from their parent's care and placed in children's homes in 1944. Mago and Thomas separated and subsequently reunited on a number of occasions throughout their troubled marriage. They had Uncle Johnnie and Auntie Teresa who were also placed in children's homes in 1952, though under very different circumstances. According to Uncle Johnnie Mago told him and Auntie Teresa one day when Johnnie was aged eight and Teresa aged six that she was taking them on an exciting trip. Mago and a female friend bundled the children into a car and took them on a long journey. When they arrived Mago made them get out, took them down a long path to a large house; and within the few moments it took for Johnnie and Teresa to wait for the door to be answered, Mago was gone. Johnnie remembers looking behind him to see his Mother running away from her children down the path back to the car.

He later joined Daddy in his children's home and didn't see his Mother again for another four years when she appeared in court to formally sign him over to the care of the state. Johnnie had a vague recollection of learning around that time that he had a half-brother named Paddy who was also deserted by Mago. Johnnie believes that he and Teresa were abandoned by Mago so she could go fruit picking in Scotland with her friend. He also recollects that they had another Sister called Annie who died aged four before they went into care.

During another reunion with Thomas, Mago had two more children with him, Charlie and Simey (ironically Charlie's second wife, whom he married many years after Mago's death, was the daughter of the friend she left her children to go fruit picking with).

Charlie and Simey both ended up in children's homes too; although their journey into institutionalisation was due to Mago becoming sick. Whilst Mago was in and out of hospital Thomas cared for the boys, but was very cruel to Simey. Wanting to be free to gallivant and womanize, Thomas had his sons put in care, but would take them out periodically when he wanted to access state benefits. It was clear from the stories they later told and the lifelong mental health issues that plagued them, that Charlie and Simey were both subjected to horrendous sexual, physical and emotional abuse in the children's homes in which the state had placed them for their care and welfare. Charlie died from respiratory failure aged 46. Simey, a beautiful boy in face and spirit fared worse than any of his siblings, he never fully recovered from the brutal trauma that was his childhood and took his own life aged 57.

I have a photo of Mago standing in the open doorway of the hospital where she died not long after it was taken; she was wearing a drab dressing gown and looked old, careworn and frail; she had my Father's face. Johnnie went to see her a short while before she passed away, and she gave him a silver American graduation ring as they parted for the last time.

When my Father paid his final visit to Mago she told him about the ring. He was convinced that Johnnie had pressured Mago into giving him the ring, but as the oldest Son, he believed it he should have gone to him.

Johnnie had a more realistic view of Mago from bitter experience. However, Daddy had an image of his Mother of Saint like proportions. When she died he was completely devastated by his grief. His only real childhood memories of Mago were witnessing Thomas beating her when he was a very small child and the time she visited him in the children's home and she lifted him up to look out the window because he needed to know what was on the other side. Consequently, the ring became a symbol of all he had lost and was a bone of contention between the Brothers for many, many years.

Johnnie was always affable and affectionate with no outward signs of anger in him; the same could not be said of my Father. Johnnie had settled in Birmingham with his young family, but would visit us in Manchester whenever he could. He and Daddy would go out to the pub full of camaraderie, but when they returned my Father would pick a fight with Johnnie every time over the ring; and Johnnie would then have it out with my Father about the terrible way he treated my Mother.

One such incident occurred on a dark and penetratingly cold night. My bedroom overlooked the back yard which was covered in a thick carpet of unblemished snow. Teresa and I watched through the parted curtains as the two Brothers armed with self-righteous resentment, hot angry breaths rising in plumes from their tormented countenances, reigned blows upon each other, fighting over a silver ring. Teresa and I were terrified for we were convinced they would kill each other. It didn't last long as Mammy was able to intervene before much blood was shed. Following that event I dreaded Uncle Johnnie visiting; though I loved him dearly and my face would shine with delight when he turned up; the fear that Daddy would one day go too far was always prevalent.

Thomas had three other children to a woman named Bridge, Carmel, Kathleen and Barney. His last child was born in the 1960s. Kughie, to a woman named Angela who Thomas beat and terrorized to an early grave. Thomas died in Ireland in 1968. He wasn't missed.

After many battles during the early years following Mago's passing; to keep the peace

Johnnie gave the ring to Daddy. My Father wore it with pride on his little finger all through my childhood; and it did give him peace in more ways than one; it also gave him a little piece of the Mother he had never really known.

Chapter 17

A Dopey Child

My poor Mother must have been in an almost constant state of distress throughout my childhood for I was always easily distracted and was forever having accidents which resulted in some quite serious injuries.

The first one I recall occurred when I was playing in the backyard at Criccieth Street with Tommy and our cousin David. I was climbing the back gate and had reached the top when David called out to me. As I turned in response I lost my grip, fell to the ground and was knocked out cold. I came to a few hours later and found myself lying on the fancy settee in the front parlour with Mammy sitting beside me, pressing a cold damp flannel to my forehead her other soft hand was gripping mine and she wore a concerned, but relieved smile upon her face. However, her relief was short lived for it wasn't long before I was at it again.

Street lamps used to be much lower in height and had small metal bars sticking out either side just below the lamp shades; and we children loved to throw a rope over them and tie the rope in a big loop half way down which we would then swing around on endlessly. On one occasion I was swinging rather too enthusiastically, fell out of the swing, wacked my head off the pavement and knocked myself out cold again. However, this time when I came to I was in the back of Uncle Son's car lying across Mammy's lap and she was crying.

'What am I going to do with my dopey child she's always falling!' she lamented.

I became suddenly nauseous and Son had to stop the car three times on the way to the Royal Infirmary Hospital, which was only a short ride away, so that Mammy could open the car door to let me get sick, it was horrible, my face felt on fire, my head was swimming and the vomiting was projectile. When we arrived at the hospital the doctor told my Mother that I might have concussion and would have to be kept in overnight for observation, Mammy and I both wailed in alarm at the news.

There were no beds available in the children's ward so I was sent to the maternity ward. Mammy had to leave me after I'd had my tea, I was inconsolable. There was a little girl in the bed next to me, but she didn't talk so I lay in my high metal hospital bed feeling terribly sorry for myself. Though curiosity soon got the better of me, as it grew dark and the dull ward lights came on I slipped out of my bed to have a little wander around. At the end of the long ward there was a TV mounted high up on a shelf suspended from the ceiling, and in front of it was a chair all ready for me. I plonked myself in it full of excited anticipation for a great night of telly, but I never got to watch a thing as all the expectant Mums fussed over me for the rest of the evening. They questioned me endlessly about my life, told me all about theirs and showered me with fruit, drinks and sweets, it was lovely. A rather stern Matron put an end to my joyful sojourn by making me go to bed at 8.30pm sharp. I cried myself to sleep longing for my Mother.

I was rudely awoken at dawn with a lumpy bowl of porridge and a glass of watered down orange juice plopped down on my tray by a tired old nurse. At lunchtime I was given a choice of blancmange or cheese and biscuits. I opted for the later as I had no idea what blancmange was and loved biscuits. However, I was bitterly disappointed when they served dry crackers instead; and looked yearningly at the wobbling mountain of pink joy the girl in the next bed to me had wisely chosen. I was given the all clear by the doctor and discharged;

alhough the fall had clearly not knocked any sense into me as it wasn't long before my next calamity.

At the end of our section of the street there was a waste piece of land that we all referred to as the Croft. Most of the kids on the street would play there for hours on end having all sorts of adventures with old wheelbarrows, tyres and almost anything else we could work our inventive magic on. I arrived one day to discover a boy named Frankie who lived directly opposite the Croft, staring at a treasure beyond my wildest dreams, an old beat up abandoned car. I remember giggling and clapping my hands gleefully. Frankie and I soon got to work in exploring the find.

We ran around opening and slamming the doors shut, but found that the boot door had an amazing sound effect as it groaned in protestation on its rusty old hinges when we repeatedly opened and shut it.

I then got behind the wheel and Frankie sat beside me in the passenger seat, and I decided to drive us all the way to Disney World. However, Frankie rudely interrupted the journey by insisting on taking over the driving. We swapped seats, but as he wasn't able to continue the trip with the imaginary narrative I demanded I soon got bored and got out of the car.

I climbed on the bonnet, jumped around a bit then pulled myself onto the roof. I was trying to get my balance and needed a grip and the driver's door was ajar so I reached across and grabbed the top of the door frame; it was at that point that Frankie slammed the door shut on my fingers. A tornado of hot burning pain shot through my body and I screamed. Frankie leaped from the car releasing my hand; I fell off the roof onto the ground. Two of the fingers on my right hand looked like they were about to fall off and were pouring with blood.

Frankie must have run to fetch my Mother, she came running and quickly assessed the damage then picked me up and rushed home with me. She went into the kitchen and returned with Shirley's old baby bath half filled with warm water which she sprinkled liberally with salt then immersed my hand in it. The water instantly turned red, the pain was so intense I was sobbing and sweating. Mammy lifted my hand from the bloodbath, wrapped it in a towel then ran to the kitchen for fresh water. She repeated the process four times before she was able to stem the flow of blood. At that stage I could see that they weren't hanging off just deeply cut. My Mother dressed them, gave me an aspirin, lay me on the settee in the parlour and covered me with a blanket. A short while later Auntie Eileen arrived; she leaned over me, stroked my hair and kissed my clammy forehead.

'Ah, the poor crater'.

As she left the room I heard Mammy say:

'Daughter what am I going to do Tommy will kill me over this?'

He didn't though, even Daddy couldn't blame her for my many mishaps and the next one to befall me was caused by an act of kindness by my Nanna Ellie. She was never a great one for fussing over her Grandchildren, but because I was her first Grandchild and also due to having proven my worth whilst on begging trips with her, she made a bit of an effort with me.

On a scorching summer's day she called at our house and told Mammy that she was taking me to the park. My Mother dressed me in my favourite silky blue dress and off we went. We headed straight for the children's play area when we arrived at the park. In those days the play areas didn't have the lovely soft spongy ground covering that they have now. Instead, each of the rides, the slide, the sea-saw, the climbing frame, the roundabout and the swings were surrounded by mean, sharp orange gravel. I started off fine on the swing with no misfortune at all, and Nanna and I had a laugh as she pushed me on the swing as high as she could until the chains started rattling, but then it all went horribly wrong.

I scrambled to the top of the slide, shuffled my bottom onto its shiny metal surface and off I went. Unfortunately I went down it at such speed thanks to my silky blue dress, that I shot past Nanna who was waiting at the bottom to catch me and landed hard on the ruthless gravel about three feet from where she stood. I felt a vicious burning sensation at the back of my thighs, but squeezed my eyes shut to prevent myself from crying.

I lied when Nanna asked me if I was alright for I wanted the fun to continue, so I boarded the roundabout with a racing heart. My Grandmother began to spin me around and around, after only a few spins I lost my grip and flew past her landing again on the merciless orange Demon. This time though, I wailed as a large section of skin along my whole left leg was burnt off. Nanna ran to me, picked me up and hugged me:

'Oh you poor crater come here to me, let's go on home now and put some ointment on your poor sores!'

Incredibly, despite being in a burning Hell of agony, I refused to leave, I was determined that my special time with Nanna Ellie would carry on. I climbed back on the roundabout, she very reluctantly spun me once more, and sure enough I slid off yet again, but that time my body flipped over and I fell flat on my face. With a bright orange nose and no skin left on my legs Nanna wisely decided enough was enough and took me home. I was too big for her to carry; and I'll never forget the torture of the sun beating down on my gravel burns as we walked home.

My Mother was no shrinking violet, she was as forthright as her own Mother in her way, but she was brought up the same way she raised me, not to give cheek to your elders. So even though her expression was one of absolute fury when she saw the state I was in, she didn't open her mouth to Nanna, but the look she gave her spoke volumes.

Mammy spent the rest of the day bathing my wounds and applying ointment. Even though I was deeply sorry for myself, my heart had gone out to Nanna when she had walked away she had looked so sad, and she probably never got over the ordeal for she never took me to the park again.

As if all this stress and worry wasn't enough for my poor long suffering Mother I then tried to break her heart by deciding to run away. During our afternoon break in school one day I asked my friend Margaret if she would like to run away with me. She looked at me with a puzzled expression, sniffed back up the customary stream of snot running toward her upper lip, and happily agreed that she would. At home time we knew our Mothers would be waiting for us at the main gate so we cunningly slipped out of the side gate and ran through the seemingly endless back entry, eventually emerging onto a strange street. We were hot and breathless, but laughed almost hysterically. We held hands and skipped down the street and onto a main road.

Walking for a further five minutes or so we came to a fairly large shopping area, well it looked large to me as I was only used to the isolated corner shops of my neighbourhood, which I later learned was Platt Lane shops in Fallowfield. Then Margaret came to an abrupt halt; she told me that she was scared and needed to go home. I made no attempt to persuade her to stay with me; instead I turned to her and said:

'That's alright Margaret you go on home now, but if you see me Mammy will you please tell her that a black man took me?'

Margaret acquiesced to my evil request and trotted off. I wandered around the shopping area full of strangers for about twenty minutes before realizing that I too was scared, hungry and homesick for Mammy. I retraced my steps as best I could and finally reached the top of my street. I saw my Mother running towards me, her long black hair trailing behind her in the breeze, oh God she was fuming I could see it in her face when she was still a hundred yards from me; I seriously considered running away again, but then she was upon me grabbing me by the shoulders and shaking me:

'Where in the name of Jesus have you been? Why did you tell Margaret to say that a black man had took you, you bad, bad girl! I'll teach you a lesson right now you wicked girl!'

She then turned me about, pulled me

roughly, though not painfully, by my ponytail to the local police station, dragged me up the steps, pushed the door open with a crash and almost threw me at the counter where an imposing desk sergeant loomed:

'Please sir in the honour of God will you lock her up in your cells she's ran away and told a terrible lie!'

I was absolutely terrified and burst into tears. The officer came around the counter, crouched down to my level and said:

'Dry up your tears young Lady, we don't allow runaway children to cry in any of our jails! You will have to say goodbye to your Mother now because you won't be seeing her for a very, very long time for being such a naughty girl!'

That was it, my knees buckled; I threw my head back and roared, then threw myself at Mammy's knees and her mercy:

'Oh please Mammy take me home, I'm sorry please don't let the wob put me in jail!'

'What do you think sir, she seems sorry for the bad ting she's done, will we let her off just this once?' asked my Mother with a twinkle in her eye.

My own eyes began twinkling too from the ray of hope beaming into them.

'Well Missus she does appear to have learned her lesson, I'm not sure though as there's always the chance she will do it again?'

'I won't Mister I won't ever do it again I promise God!'

The lovely man then scratched his head and rubbed his chin appearing to struggle with a difficult decision, then placed his meaty hand on me, it felt like there was a ton weight of rectitude upon my small guilty shoulder:

'Right Miss, this time I'm going to let you off and not put you in jail, but if I ever hear about you running away again, lying or even giving your lovely Mum cheek, I will lock you up in our coldest, darkest jail and throw the key away, do you understand me?'

I certainly did and couldn't wait to get out of there. Later that night I was woken from my peaceful slumbers by the sound of raucous laughter from Mammy and Daddy. How could they be so carefree and hard when their oldest daughter had nearly gone to jail forever with no chance of the key to get me out ever being found? These were my last pitiful thoughts before drifting off to sleep.

Chapter 18

The End

Manchester city council had great plans for Moss Side during the 1960s and early 1970s including the demolition of many of the Victorian and Edwardian terraced houses that we called home; and in so doing, destroyed the truly multi-cultural community we shared. The area had long attracted Irish settlers since the time of the potato famine in Ireland who were joined by huge waves of immigrants from the Indian sub-continent and Caribbean during the 1950s and 1960s.

I recall the building of Moss Side precinct in the late 1960s, an American style shopping mall, which stirred boundless excitement amongst the women of the neighbourhood and fear in the hearts of the local traders. Over the next few years the council served their compulsory purchase orders with the intent of clearing the slums for their ambitious regeneration of Moss Side project.

One night after another jaunt to the pub my parents came home, and Mammy gave my Father a huge tin pot to take to the local Indian restaurant for a take out. Daddy returned a short while later with the pot half filled with chicken curry and rice. The rich, spicy aromas made my mouth water. Mammy got the plates and we all tucked in.

That was when Daddy told us about the council wanting to knock all the houses down and we would have to move. Even though I was only eight years old I felt a profound sense of loss, though my parents didn't seem to be sad at all. Our house wasn't a slum by any standards, but I think they were eager for a fresh start in a new area.

We had no choice about selling our home,

but faced with the mammoth task of rehousing all the occupants who couldn't afford to buy or rent privately in other areas, the council didn't have all the power. My Father put his foot down and refused to leave until they rehoused us in Fallowfield, specifically Nantwich Road, a tree lined Road of semi-detached properties with lovely gardens, consequently, we were one of the last families to leave the street. Day by day we watched as our neighbours and friends packed up and left; leaving properties with their memories trapped behind boarded up facades until they could find a way to join their owners.

The power cuts hit due to the miner's strike in February 1972 and by that stage there were very few people left on the street. The dark, cold evenings gave the area a surreal quality with only the ghostly flicker of candlelight in the windows of perhaps a half dozen houses the whole length of the street. By the following month it was time for us to go too as my Father had won his battle with the mighty council and we were headed for the greener roads of Fallowfield.

On moving day my Father made many trips in his pickup truck removing all our worldly goods and depositing them in our new house. On the penultimate trip he took my Mother, Tommy and Shirley with him. Teresa and I were left behind sitting on an old sideboard in the living room with a fire blazing in the grate to keep us warm; and a solitary burning candle to shed a scant light on our own memories. We didn't talk much, we just leaned on each other staring wistfully into the flames of the fire, sad to be leaving our past behind us and uncertain of the future. When Daddy returned for us he put out the fire and doused the candle.

'Come on now yee two it's time to go'.

We followed him down the hallway, the sound of our footsteps echoing throughout the empty shell that had once been filled with the sounds of family living. Once out onto the street he slammed the door shut behind him, stood still for a few moments then gave the door a little rap of his knuckle:

'Goodbye old girl we'll miss you'.

We all got in the pickup and as we drove away down the desolate street I looked back over my shoulder with a huge lump in my throat. At so young an age I didn't know how I understood, though I did nevertheless; that it was the end of a way of life that we would never have again. Our community was destroyed only to be replaced by the Alexandra Park estate which became notorious for gangland activities involving drug dealing and gun crime, and put Moss Side on the world map for all the wrong reasons. The shopping precinct was a thriving resource for a few years, but became a no go area due to high levels of crime and only lasted around twenty-five years before it too was demolished.

'We left our old dark house behind us and arrived at our new one only to find it in darkness too as the electric hadn't been connected in time for the move. With excitement at last beginning to replace trepidation Teresa and I lit another candle and set about exploring our new surroundings.

The first thing we discovered was a downstairs indoor loo, no more going outside in all weathers to do our business, what a treat it was. There was a big living room with a modern gas fire, but no parlour, so Mammy couldn't save a room for best anymore, but she had a big kitchen with a built in range so I think she was happy with the sacrifice. There was an actual bathroom too, no need to fill the big old tin bath with endless kettles of hot water any longer. The three bedrooms weren't as big, and Tommy being the only boy at that time got the boxroom all to himself. Mammy and Daddy had the master bedroom and Teresa, Shirley and I had to share a double bed in the remaining bedroom.

We had chippy for tea that night with pop for we had no way of making a cup of tea as the gas hadn't been connected either. The bedrooms were freezing so Teresa and I put Shirley between us and cuddled her for warmth.

The next morning we rose early and went outside to explore. The back garden was only small with a shed in place for Daddy's tools and his new possession, a lawn mower. The front garden was also small and had a row of brown bushes lining the path beneath the front window that Daddy told us were marigolds and they would turn lovely purple and blue colours in the spring. The side garden seemed as big as a football pitch to us and had a young acorn tree in the corner. The whole garden, front and back, were surrounded by four feet high privets. Peering over the front gate we looked up and down the road which was lined by trees and grass verges; it was so posh, I thought it was beautiful and that I might come to like it after all.

My parents travelled back to their old haunts, but found some new pubs to frequent too on their nightly outings. It wasn't long before the new house was christened with domestic violence. We children were all in bed around a week after moving in when the sound of breaking glass filled me with dread again. This was followed quickly by something being banged against a wall or door and I prayed the something wasn't Mammy.

'You fucking whore I'll kill you!'

'Fuck you, you little baldy bastard, go on then, do it!'

We were all up screaming then, Teresa ran to the top of the stairs and yelled:

'Tommy, Kate stop in the honour of God, the childer are terrified!' but it didn't stop.

Mammy screamed, Daddy yelled and it seemed that everything in that living room was being beaten and smashed. Teresa and I ran downstairs and pushed the door open with great difficulty; we squeezed through and found my Mother slumped against it on the floor; the now all too familiar sight, of her hair a knotted mass surrounding a bloody nose and puffed up eyes.

'You bastard, you'll never do this to me again!' she groaned between swollen lips.

My Father was sitting back on the armchair with his head down breathing laboriously. I hated him at that moment and willed him to look up so that he could see it in my eyes, but he didn't. Teresa and I helped my poor Mother to her feet, took her into the kitchen and bathed her battered face with warm salty water. I tried to gently push her hair out of the way to enable us to get to her face easier, but it was so matted with blood, she cried out in pain. We took her up to bed passing Daddy without a word; he hadn't moved and still didn't look up.

There a was lovely family next door, the Father was called Eric. I learned that night that whether we lived in the so called slums of Moss Side or in the relatively posh Roads of Fallowfield, what went on behind closed doors stayed there; nobody called the police that night to help us either.

Eric became a good friend to our family over the ensuing years. Although he claimed that he never involved the law (the police did turn up to investigate the many incidents of domestic violence and I always believed it was Eric) he did try on a few occasions to talk my Father out of his violent ways, all to no avail.

It was Eric who came to my aid when a light bulb I was changing in the kitchen blew up in my hand when I was babysitting one night. He took me to the hospital, filled a basin with cold water in one of the waiting cubicles, immersed my hand in it and waited with me until Daddy came home from the pub, discovered what had happened and rushed to the hospital to take over. And it was Eric who drove me at night to meet the coach for my school trip to Holland not long after. Daddy came with us, but was too drunk to drive. He cried buckets as he waved me off and Eric laughed out loud.

My first day at my new primary school, St Kentigern's; which was at the top of the road and set in a pig farm before a new housing estate was built on the land; was uneventful, albeit very intimidating for me to have to start again making new friends.

Next door to Eric lived an Irish family, one of the sons, Harry, was a little older than me and frequently appeared hostile towards me for no apparent reason, he gave me dirty looks all the time. I'd been at the school for only a few weeks; and at the end of the day I started to make my way home alone, Tommy had already raced off, when Harry confronted me:

'Hey you, dirty Gyppo, your Mum wears loads of make-up and you're a dirty Gyppo!'

I was instantly incensed by the insult to my lovely Mother who I knew only wore a little black eyeliner and lipstick when she was going out. I had a blue canvass case that carried all my school books, and was suitably heavy for the task in hand; I swung it hard against his head and was rewarded with immediate gratification when I saw that he didn't look quite so tough after my righteous wallop, and he ran off home crying all the way; though as an act of bravado he kept shouting over his shoulder all the way down the road;

'Gyppo, Gyppo, Gyppo!'

Badly shaken by the encounter I was hot in the face and breathing hard as I hurried towards home; thinking over what he'd said, trying to make sense of it, but I wasn't yet nine years old and I couldn't. I walked through the back door to see Mammy preparing dinner, she could see right away that something was wrong and rushed over to me.

'Mary what's happened, what's the matter?'

I just stood there for a few moments then said:

'Mammy, that boy next door to Eric, the one with the frizzy hair, said you wear too much make-up and called me a Gyppo, what's one of them Mammy?'

My Mother had the saddest look in her eyes as she bent towards me then wrapped her arms around me.

'Ah baby, don't let that nasty boy upset you he's not worth it. It just means you're a traveller, but you know you are, Gyppo is just a bad word for it that's all. Some bad people just don't like us and you have to get used to it baby, but if you don't tell people where you're from they won't know and can't treat you differently'.

Standing with my face nestled against my Mother's shoulder, wrapped in her arms, I felt safe, but something changed for me that day; I'd reached another end; this time it was the end of an innocence that had believed I was the same and just as good as other children, and the beginning of a feeling of insecurity and low self-worth that became an integral part of me. But we travellers are made of hardy stuff, although we face discrimination throughout our lives, we learn to cope with it by developing resilience, compassion for others and a great sense of humour, for laughter is the balm that has always soothed our troubles.

As for Harry, he rarely had a days' peace from me following his outburst of bigoted abuse; I teased him mercilessly for the rest of his primary school days about his frizzy hair and gangly legs, he at least, never called me a Gyppo again!

Afterword

Around a year after we moved to Fallowfield my wonderful Granddad Arthur died aged 58 following a long battle with respiratory illness; and this life changing event quickly led to another as Teresa had to leave us to move back in with Nanna. I missed her and Granddad terribly; and struggled for quite a while to adjust to my new found responsibility of head babysitter for my younger siblings; I felt far too young at age nine for the burden.

My responsibilities increased when my Mum gave birth to my Brother Jason on March 16th 1975, whom I later grew to love as if he were my own child. When I was 14 my Mum had a miscarriage in the kitchen in front of me, she recovered well, but didn't have any more babies after that.

My parents separated in 1984 when Mum

threw Dad out; and he then rented a council flat in Hulme for about a year until he was rehoused in a flat close to Nantwich Road, on the estate that had once been the pig farm in front of my old primary school. The domestic violence had finally ended; and my parents actually became good friends once he'd moved out. He called each day to help Mum around the house as she had very painful arthritis which limited her mobility.

A couple of years later Nanna moved to a cottage flat near Mum as she was struggling to manage living on her own in Hulme; and it was around this time that I got a cottage flat of my own in Withington. Nanna still liked to go to the pub every night, but wasn't safe to go out unsupervised; so Jason would call at her flat every night to take her in a taxi to the Claremont pub, then pick her up again after a few hours and make sure she got home safely, it was a considerate thing for a young teenage boy to do, and it brought him very close to Nanna; though she became increasing frail and eventually wasn't able to go out at all, and was mostly bedridden.

Uncle Jim still had his base with her at that time and banned her from smoking her beloved Park Drive cigarettes in bed. However, Ellie was always stubborn and had craftily stashed a few, together with a box of matches; her sneaky fag was to be her last. She had waited until Jim went out one evening before lighting up and must have fallen asleep in bed; the smouldering cigarette set fire to the flat and Ellie died later that night from the effects of smoke inhalation. We all mourned the loss of our formidable matriarch for a very long time.

My Brother Tommy has one son, Shirley has one daughter, and Jason has two daughters and one son. My siblings have battled with mental health, drug and alcohol issues all their adult lives; and in some ways they've been tough and put up a brave front; though I have no doubt in my mind that their issues arose because of the experiences of many, many years of domestic abuse and the bigotry of others.

Our Tommy grew into a complex man, who could be moody and introvert one minute, and the next have us all in stitches laughing with his ironic observations and quips, he had a wonderfully dry sense of humour. Tommy died September 18th 2000, the day after his 36th Birthday from complications arising from an enlarged heart; a condition that was present from birth, but had gone undetected all his life.

Our whole family were completely devastated and were still in the darkest depths of our grief when Mum was diagnosed with terminal cancer, she died 11 days later on November 28th 2000 aged 56, just 10 weeks after we lost Tommy. My own daughter was just under two year's old at the time. My Mother had always been my best friend; and I've never come to terms with losing her, though having my own daughter grow into a lovely young woman, and the wonderful relationship we share has helped to fill the gap left by my truly remarkable Mother.

Our beloved Auntie Eileen, Daughter, died two years after Mum, she had missed her sister Kate so much, and had never been the same without her.

All of us were profoundly affected and changed by losing Mum and Tommy, but Dad took it the hardest. He had found a companionship with Mum for over 15 years before she passed away; and although they lived separately, he told her every day how much he loved her and how sorry he was for the pain he caused her, but he couldn't take it back and could never atone for what he did. Only a few of the incidents of abuse are told herein, and Dad had to live with the knowledge and his guilt for those actions for the rest of his days.

Losing Mum and Tommy brought us all even closer than before. I found my peace with my Father, and we even became good friends; I forgave him because I recognised that he was truly remorseful for the things he had done, but he never forgave himself and was a soul in torment. He was so supportive to his family and couldn't do enough for us and the many elderly disabled people he helped in the community. I believe my Father was essentially a good man who had done some very bad things, but he lived a kinder way when he stopped denying the awareness and insight into his behaviour that he had always had. Dad died February 18th 2006 aged 65 from a cardiac arrest, his children, grandchildren and the many others who loved him were heartbroken. I like to think he left to take Kathleen home again to where her heart will feel no pain.

For most of my adult life I have worked in supportive roles, including four years in a women's refuge for the amazing Stockport Without Abuse domestic abuse service.

Only Teresa and I recall the memories of Criccieth Street vividly. Nantwich Road is still our home over 45 years later; and now has a fourth generation of our family living there. Shirley's daughter Rachel succeeded the tenancy when Dad passed away, she subsequently bought the house, and now has beautiful baby girl of her own. This time the memories can stay right where they belong.

About the author

Mary Margaret Doherty lives in South Manchester, England (she never strayed far from her roots) with her husband, teenage daughter and Gracie the cat, also known as Baba G.